Successful Shooting

BY BILL PULLUM
& FRANK T. HANENKRAT

**A PUBLICATION OF
THE NATIONAL RIFLE ASSOCIATION**

NRA BOOKS — Bill Askins, *Director;* Ted Bryant, *Editor;* Mike Fay, *Production Chief;*
Betty Bauser, *Art Director;* Cover Photo — William Parkerson.
A Division of **NRA Publications,**
George Martin, *Executive Director.*

Foreword

The United States has dominated International Rifle Shooting in the World since 1964. There has been much conjecture and speculation by the shooting fraternity as to the reason for this success so the dominance could be transferred to the shotgun and pistol disciplines and continued in the rifle events. There are several reasons recognized for the outstanding success of our rifle shooters. One very important reason is the excellent junior and collegiate marksmanship rifle programs sponsored by the National Rifle Association, which exists on a much smaller scale in the other disciplines. This has given us a much larger base of shooters from which to pick our international entries. An equally important reason was the formation of the military marksmanship units and their contributions to coaching, instruction and training of the top junior and collegiate shooters who have entered the military during the last 20 years. The United States Army Marksmanship Training Unit located at Fort Benning, Georgia has been the most successful of these units. A small handful of extremely dedicated, well trained army shooters have accounted for approximately 90% of the medals won by the United States in International Shooting Competition since it's inception. The Army Marksmanship Unit's training has not been limited to rifle shooters. They have trained many shooters in the other disciplines as well, but not with the success achieved by the rifle shooters. In my opinion, this was due to one other important factor and advantage the rifle shooters have had over the shooters from the other disciplines. This was the contact with and the coaching of Bill Pullum, who was the head coach of USAMU's International Rifle Section from 1963-69. Rifle shooters he has coached have won 11 Olympic medals and many world individual and team championships. Nearly all of the World Class rifle shooters in the United States in the past 17 years have been directly or indirectly coached by this man. I have had close contact with and have been coached by Bill Pullum since 1963.

I doubt if there is any other individual who has made such a profound impact on the shooting sport in the United States. Although not an exceptional competitive shooter in his time nor an outstanding technical coach, he was a tremendous psychological coach. He trained us to use mental discipline and convinced us that winning scores were first produced in the mind. He had an uncanny ability to derive the maximum from each of us. He taught us to constantly analyze our shooting performance and our problems, which required us to learn to think for ourselves. He treated everyone as an individual, recognizing each had different problems and each must be solved individually. Under his tutelage we developed confidence in our ability to perform, believe in ourselves and react positively under pressure. In short, he taught us to think like winners, act like winners and be winners. Many of the shooters he trained are still winning medals for the United States and attribute their success to the positive attitude formed in their relationship and contact with him.

This is Bill Pullum's and Frank Hanenkrat's second book on shooting. Frank as an Army Lieutenant in the mid sixties was assigned to the Army's Marksmanship Unit as a shooter-instructor and worked for Bill Pullum. He never developed into a world class competitive shooter, but he did recognize Bill Pullum's ability to motivate and mold many of the more promising of his young charges into world class competitive shooters. He aspired to become a writer and convinced Pullum that there was a need for a book about sport shooting. They conspired, utilizing his writing ability and Pullum's ideas, expertise, and experience to write their first book "Position Rifle Shooting" which was written primarily for rifle shooters. The book has become recognized by shooter athletes throughout the world as the "Shooters

Bible" and is considered to be the best of its kind in existence. This second book was written with a more practical, lower level theme in mind and for shooters in all of the disciplines. It complements the first and now gives the shooters the most comprehensive and technical writings about the competitive shooting sport ever published.

My success as a competitive shooter can be directly attributed to the teaching, coaching and influence of Bill Pullum. If you aspire to become a better competitive shooter or have a goal to become a world class shooter, I heartily recommend you read and re-read both books. Your training program will not be complete without them.

Lieutenant Colonel Lones Wigger

Preface

ny normal person can learn to shoot accurately. Successful shooting comes of learning basic principles and then putting them to use through practice.

There have been many systems for teaching marksmanship over the years, many of them quite elaborate and complicated. Most proposed long, unwieldy lists of fundamentals which the student was instructed to memorize and sustain in his mind while shooting. The results of these methods was more often discouragement than success.

In planning this book, we recognized that a completely new system of teaching marksmanship was needed, a system that emphasized simplicity without sacrificing thoroughness or validity. After much careful thought, analysis, discussion, and testing, we succeeded in reducing the basics of marksmanship to two fundamentals. The result, we believe, is a system for teaching and learning marksmanship that is immeasurably more effective and sound than any other system yet devised. It is a universal system, applicable to shotgun, handgun, and rifle.

The system is based on our years of research and experience at the United States Army Marksmanship Unit, an organization that has produced more world-record holders and gold medal winners in shooting sports than any comparable organization in the world. But while we emphasize target shooting in the latter half of the book, the basics of marksmanship discussed in the first half are applicable to all types of shooting situations—hunting, law-enforcement, military, recreational, what-have-you.

The simplicity of the system makes it appropriate for beginners, but this book is not directed exclusively to novices. We plan to write, at some later time, a book especially for junior marksmen. This book, while it begins with the basics,

Successful Shooting

details a complete system of instruction that will carry the shooter to the most advanced stages of development. We discuss all sides of marksmanship, from equipment selection to position building to training and coaching. The result, we hope, is a reference book that any shooter or coach can read with enjoyment and refer to time and again.

Good shooting!

William C. Pullum
Frank T. Hanenkrat

Table of Contents

1
Recoil and Related Esoterica

L ittle Johnny, age 12, went from the big city to spend two weeks on his grandfather's farm. During his stay he met a boy from a neighboring farm, 15 year old Buck, whom he regaled with stories of the constant danger of getting mugged on city streets. After a few days of listening to this, Buck, chewing on a toothpick, said, "Come on down tomorrow to where the pasture fence crosses the creek, an' I'll teach you how to deal with them muggers."

Next day Johnny showed up, and Buck explained that he was going to teach him to shoot a gun. He placed a tin can atop a fence post, opened a breech-loading, single-barrel 12 gauge shotgun with a 30-inch full choke barrel, inserted a 3-inch magnum shell, handed the gun to Johnny with some rudimentary instructions, and stood aside.

Johnny took careful aim at the tin can and pulled the trigger. The recoil lifted him briefly off the ground and then slammed him to earth flat on his back. When his mind cleared, Johnny stood up, handed the gun to his companion, dusted himself off, and without a word started to walk away.

"Hey, don't you want to learn how to shoot?" Buck asked.

"Naahh," said Johnny, "I'd rather be mugged."

The fact that we're amused by this story reveals how all of us, to some extent, feel about recoil—the "kick" that accompanies the firing of a gun can be damned unpleasant. And like Johnny, many people feel that learning more about recoil would be much more trouble than it's worth.

That's why we called this chapter "Recoil and Related Esoterica." The word esoterica, according to the *Random House Dictionary*, means "knowledge understood by or meant for only a select few." The select few we have in mind are the world's leading marksmen, the individuals who are recognized as "the best" with shotguns, handguns, and rifles. Part of the knowledge they share is an understanding of recoil and how it radically affects the accuracy of all hand-held firearms. So basic is recoil, in fact, that it lies at the heart of the first of only two fundamentals of accurate shooting.

You may be surprised to learn that shooting is based on two fundamentals only. Yet this is the case. Two fundamental principles support the whole of marksmanship skills, just as your own two feet support your whole body. What we'll do in the first part of this book is make you thoroughly familiar with those two fundamentals. But first we have to show you how those principles were discovered and why they're so important.

This present chapter is a kind of detective story. We'll be in search of basic, sometimes hidden information. We'll proceed by performing a series of experiments to establish some basic concepts, and then go on to use those concepts in an analysis of the relationships between recoil and accuracy. When we finish, you'll have the key that unlocks a number of shooting mysteries.

The first concepts we're going to investigate can be labeled "consistency" and "accuracy." For the time being we're going to consider that these are qualities that inhere in varying degrees in the mechanisms of guns and sight systems, not in the person who shoots a gun. Later we'll modify this idea a bit, but for now let's limit our discussion to machinery.

Our first experiment will serve to establish a concept of consistency. For convenience we'll work with a rifle because this type of gun provides the most vivid illustration of our subject. A handgun or shotgun could be used, though the illustration would be less precise and satisfactory; however, we wish to emphasize that the principles demonstrated in these experiments apply to all three categories of firearms. The application of the principles may differ with different guns, but the principles remain the same.

Experiment 1. Let's imagine that we have a .22 target rifle from which we've removed the stock and sights. We're left with the essential parts of any gun—a barrel, an action, and a trigger. We place this gun in a heavy, specially designed armorer's vise that will hold it absolutely rigid. The vise is arranged so the gun points toward a target 50 meters away. There are no adverse weather conditions to affect the trajectory of bullets fired from the gun.

We now select a good match-grade ammunition and carefully fire 10 rounds through the gun. An examination of the target reveals that all 10 rounds passed through the target at nearly the same point, forming a group that measures .25 inches across.

Experience tells us that this particular gun-ammo combination has very good consistency—that is, when the gun is fired at a fixed aim-point, the bullets consistently strike at or near the same point.

In its most basic formulation, consistency is repeatability. If the bullets had formed a group of one, two, or more inches across, we would say that the gun had poor consistency. Guns in fact vary widely in consistency, and later in the book we'll discuss some of the reasons why. But for now, let's continue our experiments with this same highly consistent gun.

Experiment 2. The purpose of this experiment is to establish a concept of accuracy. Accuracy refers to the capacity of a sight system to indicate the exact point where a bullet will strike a target.

We now mount a telescopic sight on the rifle in the vise, being careful not to disturb the gun or vise in any way. When we look through the scope we see that the crosshairs show an aim-point 2 inches above the group of bullet holes. We fire more rounds through the gun, and find that the bullets still group at the same point on the target, 2 inches below the crosshairs. At this point we turn the adjustments on the scope until the aim-point indicated by the crosshairs coincides perfectly with the impact point of the bullets.

This adjustment is called calibrating, and, under the special conditions created by the vise, it means that at some fixed distance from the sight system, the straight line of vision established by the sight system intersects the curved line of bullet trajectory. In this case, of course, the point of intersection is the vertical plane of the target.

We now replace the old target with a fresh one and fire 10 more rounds through the gun. This time we find the bulletholes forming a group perfectly centered on the aim-point indicated by the crosshairs of the scope.

What we have demonstrated here is accuracy—we have a sight system which enables us to visually select an aim-point on the target and predict with a high degree of certainty that the bullet will impact precisely at that point. Accuracy, then, in its most basic formulation, is predictability.

Please keep in mind that a high degree of accuracy is achieved only when two separate conditions are met. The first condition is that accuracy is possible only if the gun possesses a high degree of consistency. And the second is that there must be a precise calibration between the sight system and the gun.

Why, you may ask, is it necessary to make these distinctions? Why not limit the discussion to accuracy, which, we can all agree, *implies* the existence of a degree of consistency in the gun?

The answer is that we must keep this distinction in mind in order to understand what happens to our gun when it is removed from the rigid vise and placed in the hands of a shooter. A couple of experiments will show why.

Experiment 3. We now remove the gun from the vise and bed it carefully in a stock. Then we clamp the stock in another specially designed, heavy, vise-like machine called a cradle. We remove the telescope, for we're only interested in establishing that the gun has retained its consistency. We fire more rounds through the gun and confirm that bullet groups on the target remain quite small—about .30 inches across. In short, the bedded gun still has a high degree of consistency, though a small degree of consistency has been lost by transferring the gun from a vise to a stock and cradle.

Experiment 4. Now we remove the gun from the cradle, replace the telescopic sight, and hand it to an athlete who possesses extraordinarily good eyesight and eye-hand coordination. He gets into the prone position, fires a few rounds to recalibrate the sight system, and begins shooting 10-shot groups on the target. All conditions remain the same—we are firing the same ammo and there are no wind conditions to affect the bullets.

The shooter reports that he squeezes off each shot only when the crosshairs are centered precisely on the target, and we grant that this is in fact true. But now, the 10-shot groups have expanded to a diameter of 3 to 4 inches.

How can this be? The gun, we know, possesses nearly perfect consistency. The telescopic sight we believe to be calibrated and reliable. Yet accuracy—i.e., predictability—has been lost. Why?

Although the loss of accuracy may seem quite puzzling at first, we find a possible explanation when we begin thinking about the sequence in our experiments: we have proceeded through a progressively less rigid system of supports for the gun.

In the first two experiments, the gun was locked rigidly in a vise. In the third, the gun was placed in a stock and the stock was locked in a cradle. We cannot expect the grip of the stock upon the gun to be as rigid as the grip of the vise, and in fact it is not. When the gun was transferred to the stock, the bullet groups expanded from .25 to .30 of an inch, a factor of .05 of an inch at 50 meters. This is not a terribly significant expansion, but it is nevertheless measurable.

The major loss of rigidity occurred, however, in experiment 4 when we placed the gun in the hands of the athlete; for the human body, even in the prone position, cannot begin to approximate the rigidity of a strong metal vise. And it was at this point in the experiments that the gun lost its accuracy: with the crosshairs centered on the target, the groups expanded by 10 to 13 diameters to 3–4 inches, a tremendously significant factor.

Before we accept the loss-of-rigidity hypothesis, however, we decide that we'd better test the gun again to make sure it's still consistent.

Experiment 5. We clamp the stock in the cradle again and begin firing test groups. We discover that the groups still average .30 of an inch, but when we look through the sighting scope we discover that the groups do not coincide with the aim-point indicated by the crosshairs. Once again the aim-point is about 2 inches above the bullet holes.

This suggests that the scope may be unreliable, so we recalibrate, put up a fresh target, and continue firing test groups. The groups continue to average .30 inch, and the telescope seems completely reliable. The necessity to recalibrate strikes us as curious, however, and we make a note of this fact for future consideration.

At this point we attempt to draw a tentative conclusion about the meaning of our series of experiments. This is an important step, we know, for if the tentative conclusion is not accurately stated, or if it is based on false assumptions, it could lead our future investigations off into completely wrong and fruitless paths. We try to state the conclusion as simply as possible. After some careful thought and some revision of the wording, we come up with a single, simple statement that summarizes what we believe we have witnessed:

The loss of accuracy appears to be related to the loss of rigidity with which the gun is held.

The simplicity of this statement seems almost simple-minded, doesn't it? But in scientific investigations, basic assumptions frequently have this simplicity. Since these assumptions determine the direction of future investigations, the quality of simplicity is highly desirable.

We must now ask the question, if our hypothesis is correct, why is it correct? If the trigger is pulled each time only when the sights are centered perfectly on the aim-point, why do the bullets not strike the same aim-point? Could it be that something—something related to the loss of rigid support—happens to the gun between the time the trigger is pulled, and the time the bullet actually leaves the barrel? To answer this, we begin to investigate the mechanisms of guns and ammunition, and we learn that there are actually three well-defined time lags between trigger release and free trajectory. They may be summarized as follows.

1. Lock time. In all conventional guns, the firing pin is driven forward by a compressed spring. When the gun is "cocked," the firing pin is retracted against the pressure of the spring and held in position by a metal sear. The trigger contains a mechanism which unlocks the sear and frees the pin to be driven forward by the spring. When the trigger "breaks"—i.e., disengages the sear—there is a tiny delay in the beginning of forward travel by the pin; this delay is caused by inertia and friction acting on both the pin and spring. Furthermore, after the pin begins to travel, time is required for it to travel forward and gather enough momentum to strike the cartridge primer with sufficient impact to cause ignition. The time interval between trigger break and primer strike is called lock time, and it varies widely among different guns. We will arbitrarily assign a lock time of .07 of a second to illustrate our discussion.

The easiest way to observe lock time is with an *unloaded* revolver. Cock the hammer and pull the trigger; the hammer falls rapidly, but there is an observable time interval between the beginning of hammer travel and its conclusion.

2. Ignition time. When the firing pin strikes the primer, it condenses the primer and raises the temperature high enough to reach a flash point and cause a tiny explosion. The explosion ruptures the opposite side of the primer, sending a flash of hot, burning gas into the cartridge proper and igniting the powder charge. The charge does not burn instantaneously, but progressively (gunpowder is described not as an explosive, but as a propellent). As the powder burns it is converted from a solid to a rapidly expanding gas. The time lag between the primer flash and the complete conversion of solid powder to expanding gas, is called ignition time and may vary widely, depending on the type of primer and the type and amount of powder and its condition. Again, assuming we are working with a rim-fire .22 cartridge, we will arbitrarily assign an ignition time of .01 of a second.

3. Barrel time. When the gas begins to expand inside the cartridge case, it exerts pressure in all directions. Eventually the pressure becomes great enough to begin pushing the bullet forward through the barrel. During the travel of the bullet, two inertial and two frictional forces must be overcome. The force of the gas must overcome the inertia of the bullet at rest by imparting to it a forward velocity; the friction created by the grip of the cartridge case upon the bullet; the friction of the lands inside the barrel, which may grip the bullet tightly enough to cut grooves into it; and the inertial resistence of the bullet to horizontal spin imposed by the twist of the lands. The cumulative resistance to forward movement is considerable, as anyone knows who has ever tried to force a bullet through a rifle barrel with a cleaning rod, an exercise almost guaranteed to damage both the rod and the barrel.

In firing, the bullet does not travel from chamber to muzzle at a constant speed; it begins from a velocity of zero and accelerates until it leaves the barrel. If we measure the speed just after it leaves the barrel, we measure what is called muzzle velocity. The muzzle velocity is the highest speed the bullet will usually reach, because the accelerating force of the gases driving the bullet is lost almost as soon as the bullet leaves the barrel, whereupon the bullet almost immediately begins to decelerate as a result of air resistance.

Muzzle velocities vary widely from gun to gun and with changes in ammunition. A .45 pistol bullet may leave the muzzle traveling at about 600 or 700 feet per second (fps). Some high speed rifle bullets may attain muzzle velocities in excess of 3000 fps.

In our case, we find that our match grade rimfire .22 bullets have a muzzle velocity of just over 1080 fps. We'll assign an arbitrary barrel time of .05 of a second.

The times we assigned to each of these processes are arbitrary and may in fact vary considerably from actual measured times. However, our purpose here is not to indicate actual measured times, but to illustrate that a time lag exists between trigger break and free trajectory. The values we've assigned to lock time (.07), ignition time (.01), and barrel time (.05) give a cumulative total of .13 of a second—a considerable amount of time when you consider that most people can easily break a second into tenths by counting rapidly and silently from one to ten. The .13 second figure is not unreasonable for a rim-fire, low velocity rifle cartridge, or for low velocity rounds fired from a shotgun or revolver.

So we conclude that it is possible to fire a gun—i.e., break the trigger—with the sights centered perfectly on the aimpoint, but have the position of the gun change, perhaps significantly, before the bullet leaves the barrel and attains free trajectory. This movement could have an appreciable affect. If you establish the chamber of the gun as the center of a circle with a radius which extends 26 inches to the muzzle, and you pivot the gun from the chamber so the muzzle moves ¼ of an inch, you change the aim-point (and impact point) at 50 meters by about 19 inches. Only a minute movement is required of the gun before free trajectory is obtained in order to move the impact point an inch or two at 50 meters. As target distance increases, so does the effect of barrel movement.

We can now return to the problem raised by our experiments. In considering the possibility of gun movement before free trajectory is obtained, we can think of two possible sources of movement. One is that the shooter himself may be moving the gun between trigger break and free trajectory. In reality this is a frequent occurrence, and we will devote considerable attention to it in a later discussion of stability in shooting positions. For our purposes here, however, we are going to proceed on the basis that we've observed the shooter, discussed his self-analysis of his shots, and concluded that he's not destabilizing his body and imparting motion to the gun. While this assumption might be questionable in ordinary circumstances, for our shooter it holds valid.

That leaves a second possibility: motion is being imparted to the gun between trigger break and free trajectory by the forces of recoil. To confirm this idea we realize that we must first understand what recoil is and how it works. This leads us to a consideration of some basic principles in physics. And this is what we learn.

Recoil is an illustration of Newton's third law of motion, which states that the action of every force is accompanied by an equal and opposite reaction. In the case of firing a gun, the expanding gas which pushes the bullet down the barrel with a certain force is also pushing the gun in the opposite direction with an equal force.

The principle is not unlike that of a jet engine. A jet engine takes air into a chamber, heats it and causes it to expand, and then allows it to escape to the rear. The expansive force that pushes the air to the rear also pushes the engine forward, creating thrust. That thrust, in effect, is a continuous recoil and its efficiency in powering jet aircraft is obvious. (Remember poor Johnny being knocked off his feet?)

This explains what recoil motion is. Now we need to discover how this motion can have an effect upon firearm accuracy. Newton's first law of motion supplies the answer. This law states that a body at rest remains at rest, and a body in motion remains in motion with a constant speed along a straight line unless acted upon by an outside force.

We can see that the bullet and rifle remain at rest in relation to each other until the force of expanding gas becomes great enough to overcome their inertia. Since the bullet is much lighter than the rifle and has less resting inertia, it begins moving first; but the rapidly expanding gas quickly generates enough force to overcome the inertia of the rifle and set it in motion in the opposite direction. It is safe to assume that in any conventional firearm, recoil begins after the bullet has begun to move down the barrel but before it has cleared the muzzle.

The force of recoil imparts a rearward motion to the gun in a direction that coincides with the axis of the bore. Newton's law tells us that the gun will continue to move along that line unless acted upon by some outside force. The outside force is quickly applied in the form of resistance, which, when we examine the shape of most guns, we perceive is not coincident with the line of recoil motion. In most rifles and shotguns, the buttplate meets the shoulder well below the axis of the bore because of the drop in the stock. The stock, then, creates lines of resistance that, during recoil, push upward against the gun, causing the muzzle to be thrust upward. With most conventional handguns, the lines of resistance created by the handgrips approach the gun at an even sharper angle and the resulting jump of the muzzle is commensurately more pronounced.

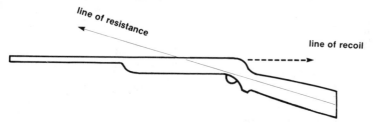

As we consider the nature of the lines of force created by resistance to recoil, we soon realize that recoil motion can readily be altered in any direction simply by changing the placement of resistance. If, for example, we are using a rifle with a conventionally dropped stock, and we cant the rifle 90 degrees to the right, the buttplate is no longer directly below the axis of the bore, but 90 degrees to the left of it. The lines of force resisting recoil will now push the gun not vertically upward, but 90 degrees to the right, placing the gun in an entirely different aim-point (toward 3 o'clock) by the time the bullet leaves the barrel.

The more we think about this, the more complex it becomes. Since it is possible to create an infinitely variable number of lines of resistant force, it is also possible to have, within the limits of energy created by the powder charge, an infinitely variable number of different recoil motions.

We find that in shooting a free rifle, for example, the position and pressure of the forward hand, if changed, could affect recoil; so could the tension in the sling or the position of the palm rest, the position and tension in the trigger hand, the position and pressure of the cheek against the stock, the position of the buttplate against the shoulder, the type of clothing worn, and the position and resistance of the entire body. Many of the same considerations could also be applied to a shotgun.

With a handgun, recoil motion could be varied by alterations in the position and tension of the hand on the grips, the angle of the wrist, the angle of the elbow, the angle of the arm from the shoulder, or the position of the entire body.

And in every normal instance where recoil motion is varied, accuracy is affected simply because recoil motion changes the aim-point of the gun before the bullet clears the barrel. The effect is less pronounced in guns with very fast lock, ignition, and barrel times, and is most pronounced in guns with relatively slow times. (It is erroneous to conclude, however, that a high-speed cartridge will improve accuracy by escaping more quickly from the barrel and hence from the effects of recoil. In some instances this may be true, but in other instances it will not be true for reasons that are too complex to discuss here.)

We are now in a position to understand accuracy in an

entirely new way. Remember we said earlier that accuracy is predictability, and that it depends upon a fixed relationship in which the straight line established by the sight system intersects the curved trajectory of the bullet at a given distance. Yet we can now see that this is true only in the very special instances where recoil motion is reduced to zero, as when a gun is held rigidly in a heavy vise.

In all other instances where recoil motion is normally present, we find that an accurate sight system is calibrated to the aim-point of the gun at the moment the bullet leaves the barrel *during recoil.* In other words, the sights are adjusted to compensate for recoil motion.

But since we have seen that there can be an infinite number of different recoil motions, and the sights are obviously calibrated for only one particular recoil motion, we are forced to reformulate our concept of accuracy.

Accuracy is predictability which depends upon gun consistency and recoil consistency. In a moment, we'll refine the statement still further.

Additional reflection reveals that this statement is extremely useful and elegant. A statement is said to be elegant if it very simply explains a complex set of phenomena. (Perhaps the most elegant of all scientific statements is Einstein's $E = MC^2$.)

The statement explains many of the mysteries that occur in shooting. It enables us to understand why, if we calibrate a sight system while shooting from a bench rest, and then pick up the gun and shoot it from an offhand position or while resting it against the side of a tree, the sights will not be accurate at all because the recoil motion will be different. We now know why sight calibrations change dramatically when we move through the prone, kneeling, and standing positions —the recoil motions are different in each position.

We can understand now why a handgun's accuracy seems to disappear when we switch from a one-hand firing position to a crouched, two-hand firing position.

We can understand why our shotgun patterns fail to touch

birds when we shoot markedly across or out of our normal positions, even though the sight picture and lead seem perfect.

We can understand why one person can calibrate the sights on a gun and strike matches with it at ten paces, and another person shooting the gun with the same sight setting won't even come close.

At this point our hypothesis seems very elegant and useful, but as scientists we need to verify it by a hard-nosed empirical test.

Experiment 6. The same gun used in our other experiments is given back to our athlete-shooter, who will operate under the same conditions. As an ideal athlete, the individual is extremely coachable and can do just about anything humanly possible if properly instructed.

We explain to him that he constitutes a support system for the rifle, and that he must keep all points of contact between himself and the rifle absolutely consistent each time he shoots.

Our shooter calibrates the telescopic sight and begins shooting a 10-shot course at the target 50 meters away. Immediately upon firing the fifth shot he looks up at us and says, "Uh-oh—I let that shot off when the crosshairs weren't centered."

"Where were they?"

"In the 9-ring at three o'clock."

We check through a spotting scope and see that he has called the shot accurately. He completes the course, and all the shots except the fifth are grouped tightly inside the 10-ring. Actual measurement shows the 9-shot group to be .34 inches across.

We can now make a final formulation of the concept of firearm accuracy:

Accuracy is predictability based upon gun consistency, recoil consistency, and shooter consistency.

We can put this in down-to-earth language and state it as one of only two fundamentals of shooting:

The First Fundamental: To achieve accuracy, you must hold the gun exactly the same way each time.

This means, of course, that you hold it the same way each time you shoot from a given position. It's physically impossible to hold a gun the same way in the prone and standing positions, but it is possible to hold it the same way each time you shoot in the prone position, or in the standing position.

Change the forces acting on the gun—that is, the force or placement of anything touching the gun—and accuracy may be radically affected.

At this point we can derive an important corollary from our first fundamental. A corollary is a proposition that follows logically from an already proven proposition.

Corollary 1: In order to hold the gun exactly the same way each time, you must position your eyes in the same relation to the gun each time.

This means, again, the same way each time you shoot from a single position.

Corollary 1 has the important benefit of vastly simplifying the way we are required to think about sighting and aiming techniques. Let's review the concepts of *sight picture* and *sight alignment* to see the corollary's effects.

The diagram on the left illustrates a sight picture containing an error in aim-point. The diagram on the right contains an error in sight alignment.

Both concepts are usually taught as "fundamentals" of shooting, and, quite rightly, errors in sight alignment are said to be proportionately much more serious than errors in aim-point. The problem, however, is that in designating these concepts as "fundamentals," various complications and errors are needlessly introduced; more items are added to the mental checklist a marksman must deal with each time he aims and fires, and this complicates his mental processes.

But perhaps more seriously, the concepts are not fundamentals at all. Whoever first designated them as "fundamental" was perhaps thinking something like this: "The sights determine where the bullet will strike; therefore, when you shoot, you must make certain that the sights are properly aligned."

But this reasoning contains two erroneous assumptions. First, the sights do not determine where the bullet will strike; as we have seen, the gun alone determines trajectory (given consistency in ammunition and wind conditions).

Second, sight alignment is not, as the above statement implies, merely a relationship between the front and rear sights. In fact, the relationship between the front and rear sights is mechanical and remains fixed unless the sight mechanisms are themselves moved. Sight alignment is actually a relationship between the sight system and the shooter's eye.

Sight alignment alone is not a guarantee of accuracy. It is possible for a shooter to maintain sight alignment while positioning his head back or forth almost anywhere along the visual axis of the sight system. By doing this, he can maintain sight alignment but cause radical changes in the pattern of recoil. It is of far more importance to bring the eye into a relationship to the gun and then keep that relationship constant. The sight system can then be moved, mounted in a different place on the barrel if necessary, in order to establish a new visual axis that can be adjusted for proper sight picture and sight alignment.

Thus we have Corollary 1, "In order to hold the gun exactly the same way each time, you must position your eye in the same relation to the gun each time." But actually it is not necessary to remember or think about this every time you shoot. The corollary is implied in the simplicity of our first fundamental:

To achieve accuracy, you must hold the gun the same way each time.

Simple, isn't it? Achieving this goal, of course, is more difficult than stating it, but keeping this goal in mind vastly simplifies and clarifies what you're trying to do when you shoot. We'll give you help on how to achieve this goal in the following chapters. But first, let's have a look at the second fundamental—the only other thing you'll have to know in order to shoot successfully.

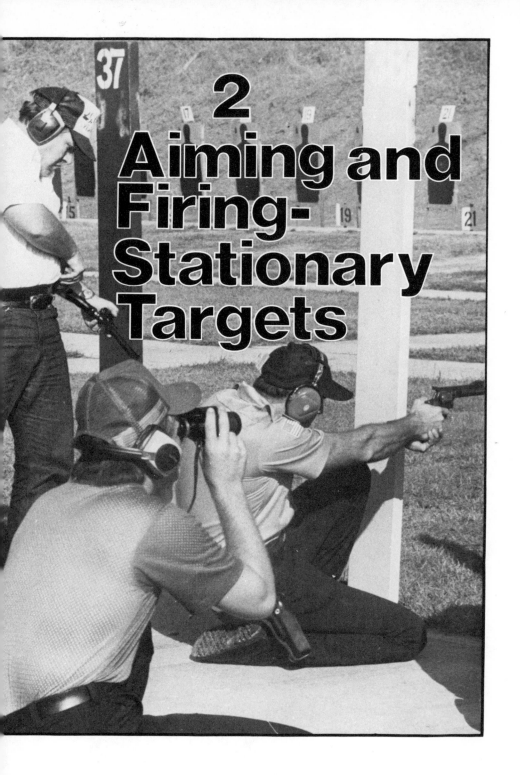

2
Aiming and Firing- Stationary Targets

I n this chapter we're going to examine the other fundamental of accurate shooting, which is:

The Second Fundamental: To shoot accurately, you must hold the gun steady while firing.

This statement has two applications—one for stationary targets and another for moving targets. For now we'll concern ourselves only with stationary targets. In this application, the statement means that the gun should remain motionless while the trigger is pulled.

We'll say right off the bat that the best way to achieve steadiness is to rest the gun on a stable support. The best example is the bench-rest shooter who rests his upper body against a heavy table and the fore-end of the rifle on a sandbag or other supportive device. Not surprisingly, bench-rest rifle shooters have the highest standards of accuracy of any form of shooting.

Hunters, law-enforcement officers, and others can readily make use of gun supports. A hunter, for example, can often rest a rifle on a tree-limb, log, or boulder. A law-enforcement officer might use the hood of a car, resting his forearms on it to support either a rifle, shotgun, handgun, or grenade gun. This technique has the added advantage of providing protection against returned fire.

It should be noted that the best supports lie directly beneath the gun. Because they affect recoil, supports usually require a recalibrated sight setting or an altered sight picture to achieve good accuracy. Only practice can tell you what the change will be.

Side support has a much greater and often unpredictable effect upon accuracy. A rifle held against the side of a tree, for example, or a handgun fired when the forearm is pressed against the corner of a building, will recoil away from the support and may throw the bullet completely wide of the target. If you anticipate having to use supports like these it would be worthwhile to practice with them to determine the effects.

If circumstances permit, another excellent way of achieving stability while aiming is to lower your center of gravity by firing from the prone or sitting positions. Most people can achieve very steady aim in either position, especially in riflery where the use of a sling can provide further help in stabilizing the gun. Experiment to find the variations of these positions that are best for you. Remember that because recoil may be different, you may have to recalibrate your sights or alter your sight picture.

In shooting from a support or a low position, try to maintain perfect stability in your body until recoil is completed. A common error is to relax somewhat when the trigger breaks, and because of the time lag between break and free trajectory, the body movement resulting from the relaxation disturbs aim.

Another common error is to impart motion to the gun through trigger pull. Don't jerk the trigger; rather, squeeze smoothly.

The use of supports and low positions is best suited to stationary or slow-moving targets, and to situations that do not require quick reaction time. If either method can be used (and they can sometimes be combined), however, they are unquestionably the best ways to achieve steady aim. This is common knowledge and we mention these techniques only because in many situations they make perfectly good sense.

Okay. But what about situations where you can't use a support or a low position? What can you do then?

We're going to reveal the secrets of this kind of shooting —the esoterica, if you will—but what should be made clear is that the principles revealed in the following pages cannot be learned simply by reading. They are principles of behavior, or performance, and they can be learned only by practice. We'll guarantee, however, that if you do practice and master them, your marksmanship ability will improve many times over, even if you shoot from a support or a low position.

To give focus to our discussion, we're going to investigate the principles involved in one of the most complex of all shooting positions: the standing position as used in international (Olympic style) free-rifle competition. This position demonstrates all the principles of aiming and firing any kind of gun—rifle, pistol, or shotgun. The application of the principles may differ from one situation to another—for example, you obviously do not hold a handgun the same way you do a rifle—but the principles involved in aiming both are the same. We'll state each principle clearly as we move through the discussion. With just a bit of thought, you should be able to see how each one applies to whatever kind of shooting you prefer. Note the distinction between principles and fundamentals. Both are basic, but fundamentals are true foundations; principles rest upon fundamentals.

In your imagination, then, come with us to the sandy, pine-covered flats of Fort Benning Military Reservation in Georgia. We'll be visiting Parks Range, home of the world famous United States Army Marksmanship Unit's international rifle team. Team members will be firing from many of the semi-enclosed booths in the 40-point sheds on the firing line, but we'll have a separate booth to ourselves. We're in a small, concrete-floored booth that opens on the rear to a spectator area and on the front to the targets.

If you're already experienced in international style riflery, most of this will be familiar to you. If not, try in your imagination to participate in this as fully as possible.

The first thing we do is outfit you with a comfortable shooting jacket and position you on a firing point. If you're a right-handed shooter, you'll be facing about 45 degrees to the right of the target, which is 50 meters away.

We now hand you a fine Anschutz model 1413 rifle. It's a .22 rimfire gun, extremely consistent, weighing approximately 17 pounds. It has a thumb-hole stock, adjustable palm-rest and butt-hook, and, just for this experiment, a 10-power scope.

We ask you to maintain an erect body position and aim at the target. You muscle the heavy rifle into position and find that you have to struggle against the weight to prevent it from pulling you forward and off balance. You must use your left arm to muscle the gun up into aiming position. In a few moments, the muscles of your left arm and lower right back begin to fatigue with the effort. If you continued in this effort, those muscles would soon begin to tremble. As you look through the scope, you find that your position is hopelessly wobbly and unstable.

At this point we ask you to bend from the waist to bring your upper torso behind and to the right of your hips. This draws the weight of the rifle in toward your feet, and at a recognizable position you discover a point of equilibrium, a position at which the combined center of gravity of body and rifle is directly over your feet. The weight of the upper torso and rifle now fall upon the bones of the lower spinal column, and the strain upon your back muscles has been removed.

We now ask you to disregard your sight picture and, the palm-rest in your left hand, to rest your left elbow and upper arm against your left rib cage, or hip-bone if your elbow reaches that low. You find that the gun now points about a foot below the target, but that the muscle strain in your left arm has been completely eliminated and the gun appears much more stable. This leads us to state our first two principles:

Principle 1. Increased stability results from good balance.

Principle 2. Where possible, the weight of the gun should be supported by bones, not muscles.

The first principle is universal—it applies to all shooting. The second cannot always be applied—as when shooting a pistol from the standing position, for example—but whenever it is applicable it should be followed.

The next thing we ask you to do is to aim the rifle at the

bull without transferring any additional rifle weight to the muscles of your left arm. To do this, you must force an increased bend to your back and force your hips further forward and to the left. You find that this introduces strain into the muscles of your back and hips.

We ask you to return to your previous balanced, more comfortable position and let the gun resume pointing beneath the target. We then adjust the palm-rest and butt-hook for you to bring the gun's aim-point onto the bull. You are now in a stable, relatively comfortable position (we say relatively comfortable because a person unaccustomed to this position finds it initially somewhat uncomfortable) with the gun pointing exactly where you want it. This illustrates principle 3.

Principle 3. The gun should fit the shooter's body and position.

The gun should fit the shooter's body. A free-rifle, with its adjustable palm-rest and stock, offers the ultimate flexibility in gun adjustments to the target shooter. In addition to adjustments, the shape and size of the palm-rest can also be varied.

Your body should not have to make extraordinary adjustments to fit the gun. To do so destroys balance and places the muscles under strain. As we shall see, the latter is an especially serious problem.

The next thing we ask you to do is to take a deep breath and exhale slowly, studying the sight picture. You do this and find that inhaling raises the muzzle, exhaling lowers it. Breath control, then, is an excellent way to make vertical adjustments in your sight picture. But you find that gun stability deteriorates when you inhale or exhale as completely as possible.

Principle 4. Stability is improved by holding a moderate amount of air in the lungs.

We now ask you to take a deep breath, let it out slowly until the sights center on the bull, then confine yourself to extremely shallow breathing and observe the sight picture. You do this, and watch the crosshairs wander around on the bull, sometimes wandering completely outside the bull. You can detect a faint up-and-down pulse in the gun that coincides with your heartbeat. We can observe the more obvious motion of the gun, of course, and ask if you're experiencing any difficulty. And you reply,

"I can't hold the gun still."

Forgive us, now, for having put you in an embarrassing situation, but we've taken a bit of creative license here to introduce a common error. Almost every beginner assumes that a steady aim results from "holding the gun still." But this puts the cart before the horse. The gun should rest comfortably on the body, and the gun is held motionless by holding the body still.

Principle 5. Gun stability results from body stability.

As simple as it is, this is perhaps the most important of the principles we will list here. There is little doubt in our minds that failure to grasp this principle is the major obstacle to learning to shoot well.

It is an easily observable fact that many shooters never learn to achieve body stability. One reason, of course, may be lack of practice. But in other cases this is clearly not the reason. No amount of attention given to "holding the gun still" will produce a steady aim. The gun will wander continuously around the bull, and the shooter will be forced to rush the trigger and shoot "on the fly" as the sights drift through the center of the bull. It's possible to acquire some skill at this through extended practice, but the results in terms of accuracy can never compare to the superior method we'll soon describe.

We'll ask you now to rest your Anschutz on the waist-high shelf across the front of the shooting booth while we enter a detailed discussion of the technique of aiming.

Aim and stability

Aiming is holding a gun so the sights remain centered on a selected point of impact.

A steady aim implies stability, or resistance to motion. If you could achieve perfect body stability you could hold a gun absolutely motionless. But the fact is that no person can do this unless he's dead and in a state of rigor mortis.

The human body, even when the skeletal portion is at rest, is in a state of constant activity: the heart beats, the blood flows, the diaphragm contracts and relaxes, air flows in and out of the lungs, the involuntary muscles of the intestines move food and liquids through the digestive tract, the kidneys move fluids to the bladder. So even if you hold yourself as still as possible, you're literally full of activity that results in small but nevertheless significant movement in your whole body.

So when you aim a gun, the involuntary muscles of your body—heart, intestines, etc.—are going to impart some motion to your body and hence to the gun. Pulsations from heartbeat are the most persistent, and will usually occur even when you're shooting from a supported position, even though you may not be able to detect the pulse unless you mount a scope on the gun.

One result of these internal activities when you're in the standing position is a slow oscillation of your body. You may sway forward slightly; nerve sensors in your head, neck, ankles, and elsewhere detect the motion and set up a righting reflex that pulls your body backward toward its center of gravity. If it drifts backward past the balance point, the same reflex mechanisms will start to pull it forward again, and the oscillating rhythm may continue indefinitely.

All shooters experience this motion in the standing position, and the better shooters learn to minimize it to the point that an observer can barely detect it. If this motion is small, slow, and steady, the shooter can learn to compensate for it by shifting his aim to the right as he drifts to the left of the target, and vice versa. Good shooters acquire this ability without being aware of it, and it appears not to be a major obstacle to a steady aim.

You can observe body oscillation, and also the reflex adjustments that compensate aim, by standing in front of a mirror and aiming at a small dot drawn on the mirror as a substitute for a target. As you aim, you will see the dot remaining centered in your sights even as your body sways, in a kind of reversed pendulum fashion, in its slow oscillation.

Your goal, of course, is through practice to reduce these oscillations to the absolute minimum. Success depends upon a continual training program that stretches over several months or even years.

So far we've talked mostly about involuntary muscles and reflex movements. Our principal interest, however, is in the motor activities of the voluntary muscles that control the skeletal system. Ordinarily we think of "using" voluntary muscles only to produce movement. In fact, just attempting to use muscles to prevent movement seems quite unnatural to most people.

To illustrate this, hold yourself as motionless as possible for one minute and observe how stressed you begin to feel. Do this now, before reading on.

Small but fairly constant motion activity seems to fulfill some need of the body. We fidget constantly, usually without being aware of it; even in sleep we move a considerable amount.

Holding the body still, then, is a type of activity to which most of us are unaccustomed, and we have to learn to do it.

Principle 6. The ability to hold the body still while shooting is a learned skill.

When first confronted with this concept, many people regard it as curious or even ridiculous. Being still, they say, is merely the absence of muscle activity. Yet when you think about it, this is obviously untrue unless you're lying relaxed on a bed, lounge, or some other surface that gives complete support to your body. If you're standing or even sitting upright and relax all the muscles of your body, you'll collapse downward. Just standing upright in the normal way, which is usually far from motionless, requires widespread muscular activity. Try observing yourself and others in normal standing situations and notice the amount of movement involved. You may in fact never see an untrained person stand still.

Standing in the upright position while supporting the weight of a gun, and standing still, requires extremely fine, continuous motor adjustment throughout your body. The motor skills involved in these adjustments must be learned, just as any fine motor skills must be learned. The fact that these skills produce no visible motion does not negate this fact. Without training, you can no more hold your body and a gun still in the standing position that you can, without training, leap from a diving board and perform two-and-a-half perfect somersaults and two full twists before knifing into the water. The skills in standing still are probably more complex and more difficult to learn.

The implication, of course, is clear: you learn to hold still through practice. We'll discuss guidelines for practice in the chapter on training. But the question we must now confront is *how* does one hold still? What is involved?

Well, obviously we're talking about the performance of the voluntary muscles, and these are subject to the control of the will. We can even pause here to state another principle.

Principle 7. Body stability is the result of conscious muscle control.

The important implication of this principle is that the mind and will, during shooting, should be engaged in sensing and controlling muscles throughout the body. It's perfectly obvious that thinking about sex or the latest news or the price of gasoline is not the kind of mental activity we're after here. Nor is thinking about what score will win the match, what will happen if you shoot a 7 instead of a 10, or even how much you want your next shot to be a 10. The mind should be engaged in sensing and controlling the body.

From here on we're going to be swimming in some murky waters, for the discussion is leading us into the question of how the mind works. And the truth is, we don't know. Nobody does.

One traditional view is that the mind is a mystical entity that exists independently of the body and brain.

The modern scientific view is that the mind is a product of brain activity and therefore has no existence independent of the brain. This view, based upon recent research findings, emphasizes the almost incomprehensible complexity of the brain. The brain contains over 100 billion neural cells linked together in a complex network involving 10 trillion neural connections. Just one cubic inch of brain tissue contains 100 million nerve cells connected to fibers which, end to end, would reach to the moon and back.

Brain activity consists of electrical and chemical impulses by which individual brain cells "talk" to one another. The level of activity is enormous. The brain consumes 25 percent of the oxygen used by the entire body. Each second, it receives 100 million nerve impulses from various sense organs. It processes all of this at the same time that it monitors and regulates scores of internal body functions; remembers; thinks; feels; and creates. The human brain is by far the most complex mass of matter yet discovered in the universe.

Some recent discoveries about the brain, we believe, have direct bearing on the subject of stability in aiming. Scientists have recently learned that the brain's two hemispheres emphasize different functions. The left hemisphere is the locus of verbal thought, of language use. As you read these words, the left hemisphere of your brain is engaged.

The right hemisphere is the locus of non-verbal mental activities such as conceptualization of form and space and integration of data supplied by the senses. To engage this portion of your brain, close your eyes and visualize as clearly as possible the following series of geometric forms: a circle; a sphere; a cube; a pyramid. Do this now, before reading on.

If you concentrated hard enough in producing these mental images, you should have found that verbal thought— thinking in words—completely ceased, or nearly so (the right hemisphere appears to have a very limited verbal ability which sometimes emerges while the brain is engaged with concepts of space and form, but the verbal sequence often has a halting or fragmentary quality).

The idea of non-verbal thinking strikes many of us as peculiar or even self-contradictory, for in Western culture we are conditioned to equate "thinking" with "words." Various Eastern cultures, on the other hand, have long been familiar with non-verbal mental states and have even devised elaborate mental exercises which are non-verbal.

But we need not go to Eastern thought to further explore this concept. We use non-verbal states frequently, without realizing it. Try these simple activities which require intense concentration on fine motor skills or on the senses, and become aware of your mental state:

Thread a needle, or perform some comparable task that requires very fine motor control.

Look at something really closely, examining its color, shape, and texture.

With your fingertips, examine some object, noting its shape, texture, and temperature.

You should find that as you concentrate intensely on these activities, verbal thinking is suspended.

In shooting, you are engaged in relationships of form and space; you are concentrating on visual and other sensory feedback; and you are exercising very fine motor control.

Your mental state, in short, should be non-verbal. The left, verbal hemisphere of your brain should be disengaged. The right, non-verbal hemisphere should be operative, sensing the sight picture, sensing the body, controlling the body muscles and the trigger finger.

Some years ago, before the discovery of the different functions of the two hemispheres of the brain, very elaborate and difficult explanations had to be put forth to deal with the non-verbal activities involved in aiming and firing. The different functions of the two hemispheres provide the basis for another elegant explanation of complex phenomena.

Without reference to the two hemispheres of the brain, we can now state the eighth principle.

Principle 8. Mental activity during aiming and firing is predominantly non-verbal.

Verbal descriptions of this mental activity are, not surprisingly, extremely difficult and always inadequate. We will not even try to give one. But fear not, you will know when you achieve this state, and by practice and repetition you will be able to achieve it more and more easily until it becomes almost automatic.

Aiming stability must be judged within two parameters. One is the actual degree of steadiness obtained. A well-trained individual can achieve a degree of steadiness in which no visible movement (with the possible exception of pulse beat) appears in the sight picture to the unaided eye. A beginner will find that this fine degree of steadiness appears very seldom; more often, the sights will appear to drift slowly about inside the 10-ring, 9-ring, or even 8-ring. But perfect apparent steadiness occurs with increasing frequency as a result of training.

The other parameter of stability is durability, or the time duration of maximum steadiness. Not even the best shooters can maintain maximum steadiness indefinitely. They can maintain it only for 3 or 4 seconds in most cases, and sometimes much less. (Remember that we are talking about the standing position. Stability improves within both parameters in lower, inherently more stable positions).

The goal of training, of course, is to achieve a degree of steadiness with no apparent motion that has a long enough duration to allow the trigger to be pulled while the sights remain centered perfectly on the target. Beginners will often think that this is not possible, except perhaps once in a hundred shots. But the scores fired by Olympic champions show that the goal really is achievable.

As an illustration, consider that the international style 50-meter target used in the Olympics has a 10-ring about the size of the iris of the human eye. The 9-ring is roughly twice as large. There is a reduced version of this target, posing the same degree of difficulty, for use on 50-foot indoor ranges where atmospheric and light conditions remain constant. A few riflemen have fired the standard 40-shot standing course on these targets with perfect scores of 400. Scores between 395 and 399 are almost commonplace among the best shooters. These people, shooting from the standing position, are giving performances that very nearly approach the consistency capabilities of their guns. They reach this level of performance by firing from nearly motionless positions. The belief is that this level of skill is primarily a product of training.

Firing and stability

Many people consider aiming as a preliminary to firing. Actually, aiming precedes but also extends through the act of firing. No muscular tension anywhere in the body should be changed until the bullet achieves free trajectory, although of course body position will be affected by recoil. The trick is to keep body response to recoil the same each time, and this is best accomplished by simply maintaining the same degree of tension in all muscles until recoil is complete.

Firing—the actual release of the shot—is of course a product of squeezing the trigger. It is imperative that the squeeze not impart motion to the gun.

Most experienced shooters touch the trigger with the fleshy pad on the tip of the index finger, where the sense of touch is most sensitive. Others touch the trigger with the joint just behind this pad, which is more firm. Use of the second or middle pad is undesirable because it exerts pressure toward the side of the gun.

Whatever touch technique you adopt for a given course of fire, use it consistently. Why? Because if you change the position or grip of your trigger hand, you may affect recoil and hence accuracy. In the standing position, the lightest possible grip consistent with a smooth squeeze is usually the best.

Most shooters prefer to take up trigger slack while establishing the aim, usually some time before the shot is actually fired.

Obviously, trigger squeeze must be integrated into the act of aiming, so we have another principle

Principle 9. Trigger squeeze should occur within the time-frame of maximum steadiness and impart no motion to the gun.

Trigger squeeze is a very delicate movement, and ideally it results from a contraction of only those muscles controlling the index finger. Other muscles controlling the rest of the hand, arm, and shoulder should not participate. Training and practice are required to learn to isolate and control this single group of muscles. Trigger pull is unquestionably a fine-motor behavior and the mental activity associated with it should be predominantly non-verbal.

The decision to fire is based upon a complex set of neural feedbacks pouring into the brain. Some come from the eye and involve judgments about sight alignment and sight picture. Others come from throughout the body and involve sensory and kinesthetic judgments about the durability of muscle control. Since all of this activity is probably centered in the right hemisphere of the brain another principle applies.

Principle 10. Mental activity during trigger squeeze remains predominantly non-verbal.

Again, we cannot adequately describe the subjective experience of this act, but you will recognize it when it occurs, or, more likely, immediately after it occurs.

People engaged in competition or in shooting at living targets may find that excitement or anxiety tend to disturb the mental activities in shooting. Excitement is indicated by accelerated heart and breathing rates, sweating armpits and hands, an adrenalin rush, and other symptoms, including increased verbal activity in the thought processes. Excitement and anxiety are both normal responses and are nothing to be alarmed about in and of themselves. However, the switchover to verbal thinking usually has a negative effect upon shooting performance. Through practice, you can learn to "shut off" the verbal hemisphere of the brain and engage the non-verbal portion. This skill is learned through mental self-discipline and practice, and we'll have more to say about it in the chapter on training.

Let's review the 10 principles we've identified:

1. Increased stability results from good balance.

2. When possible, the weight of the gun should be supported by bones, not muscles.

3. The gun should fit the shooter's body and position.

4. Stability is improved by holding a moderate amount of air in the lungs.

5. Gun stability results from body stability.

6. The ability to hold the body still in shooting is a learned skill.

7. Body stability is the result of conscious muscle control.

8. Mental activity during aiming is predominantly non-verbal.

9. The trigger should be squeezed within the time-frame of maximum steadiness, and should impart no motion to the gun.

10. Mental activity during trigger squeeze remains predominantly non-verbal.

Now here you are, still standing in a firing booth at Parks Range, and probably eager to do some shooting to see if you can apply these principles. So we'll give you just five rounds and ask you to shoot at a regulation bull 50 meters away. To simplify discussion, we'll assure you that the sights are calibrated correctly.

You raise the heavy Anschutz into position, leaning back and resting the weight of the gun and upper torso on the bones of the lower spine. You take a deep breath, exhale until the crosshairs reach the 10-ring, then begin very shallow breathing. The crosshairs wander slowly, halt, begin drifting again. You concentrate hard, trying to hold your body still, but you're still thinking in words. You draw another deep breath to supply your body with oxygen and return to shallow breathing, trying to hold your body still. The crosshairs continue to move slowly, drifting, occasionally stopping momentarily outside the 10-ring, then drifting again. You're wondering why, thinking verbally, talking silently to yourself. Finally you get the crosshairs to settle near the 10-ring, you hold your breath and rush to pull the trigger. The trigger pull disturbs the gun and the bullet hits the outer edge of the 8-ring.

This same experience is repeated three more times, with similar results. On the fifth shot, however, your consciousness is mysteriously non-verbal as the crosshairs center in the 10-ring long enough for you to squeeze off the shot during maximum stability, and the bullet strikes the center of the target. You're getting the hang of it; but just to whet your appetite, we're going to stop you at this point.

You give the gun to our assistant and we walk down the narrow concrete floor toward the exit. On the way, we stop and silently watch an Olympic champion firing a 40-shot standing course. A tripod-mounted spotting scope enables us to observe his target. As we watch, he methodically places five consecutive shots into the 10-ring.

We leave the firing shed and walk outside to stand on the grassy lawn in the sunshine. You inquire about the champion's shooting skill, and we answer more-or-less as follows.

He appears to possess no extraordinary physical abilities. His eyesight is good, perhaps slightly better than 20/20, but not nearly as acute as the eyesight of other shooters we've known. His physical coordination is also good, but again not as exceptional as that of many other shooters. What, then, accounts for his being perhaps the best rifleman in the world for a number of years?

In some sports, genetically determined characteristics such as speed, strength, or size can make some athletes superior to others. But if these differences are removed or are inconsequential, mental abilities and the state of training are the only things that separate the champions from the herd. This is true in all sports.

There is no question that the Olympic champion is exceptional. But natural physical abilities have not made him so. What makes him exceptional is the quality of his mind, his ability to engage his consciousness fully and exclusively in the act of shooting. It was through this route that he developed his physical skills. There is no reason to believe that he was born with this mental ability. He developed it through training.

The difference in shooting skills between you and that Olympic champion is probably attributable to that fact alone. Very likely, you can narrow the gap between his skills and yours just as much as you want to. Victory usually goes to the person who trains most thoroughly.

Our imaginary journey to Fort Benning is over. We leave you reading this book—and, we hope, with something to think about.

3
Aiming and Firing-Moving Targets

Everything we've said about aiming and firing at stationary targets applies also to moving targets. Moving-target marksmanship is based upon the same two fundamentals and the same ten principles (where applicable), and anyone interested in this chapter should thoroughly study the preceding chapter before continuing. In this chapter we will introduce two new principles. Little effort is required to understand them, though considerable practice is necessary to master moving-target techniques.

Let's begin with a basic concept. If you're shooting at a moving target you must "lead" the target, that is, fire ahead of it so the bullet and target reach the same point in space at the same instant. Judging the correct lead requires experience and familiarity with the target, the gun, the ammunition, and possibly the weather conditions. Two methods are used to establish the correct lead while aiming and firing.

Sustained lead. In this method, you aim initially in front of the target, select the proper lead distance, track the sight picture along at the same apparent speed as the target, and fire at any time.

Swing-through lead. In this method, you aim initially behind the target, track the sight picture along at a faster rate than the apparent speed of the target, swing through the target, and fire when the proper lead-point is reached.

In both methods, the motion of the gun should be smooth; the rate of motion should remain constant or steady throughout.

Also, in both methods, trigger pull should not disturb the steady motion of the gun and the gun should continue swinging smoothly until the completion of recoil. This continued after-motion is known in all sports as *follow-through* and is extremely important in moving-target marksmanship.

With these ideas in mind, let's return to *Fundamental One: to achieve accuracy, you must hold the gun the same way each time.* We know why this is important—it affects recoil. But how do we apply it in moving-target shooting? The answer is simple, and can be stated as a principle.

Principle 11. In tracking the target, the entire upper torso should pivot above the hips.

Observing this principle allows the shooter to maintain, within the limits of possibility, the same relationship between gun and body and thereby minimize changes in recoil. Since different kinds of weapons involve different stances and body positions, let's examine the basic mechanics of different types of shooting and see how this principle applies.

Handgun. In one-hand style, the shooter aims with the gun-hand extended forward and angled at about 70–90 degrees from the body; the opposite hand rests in a pocket or in the hip or belt; weight is distributed evenly on both feet, though possibly an individual might prefer to distribute his weight unevenly. To track the target, pivot the entire upper torso above the hips.

In two-hand style, the shooter aims while holding the gun in both hands, which are extended directly in front of the body; legs are bent and the body is in a comfortable (not exaggerated) crouched position; weight is distributed evenly on both feet. To track the target, pivot the entire upper torso above the hips.

Shotgun and rifle. A right-handed shooter faces about 45 degrees to the right of the target; the left knee may be slightly bent and the left foot may bear up to 60 percent or more of body weight; the torso may be bent slightly forward from the hips. To track the target, pivot the entire upper torso above the hips.

Running-game competition. In running game competition, the target moves across a fixed distance and rules do not allow the competitor to assume his aiming stance before the target appears. To adapt to moving targets, simply pivot the entire upper torso above the hips while tracking the target.

In any type of shooting in which the gun is brought rapidly into the aiming position after the appearance of the target, mounting the gun and tracking the target should constitute a single, fluid motion, and not two separate motions.

Now we're ready to apply the second fundamental: *To shoot accurately, you must hold the gun steady while firing.* Obviously, when applied to shooting at motionless targets, this statement means that the gun remains motionless. Applied to moving targets, however, it means that the gun tracks steadily along the trajectory of the target without unnecessary movement. The rate of the tracking motion may or may not coincide with the apparent angular motion of the target, as we've seen in the discussion of sustained and swing-through tracking. But in either case, we can apply this principle.

Principle 12. In tracking the target, gun motion should be smooth and steady until the completion of recoil.

If you think about this principle for a moment you'll realize that it's little more than a paraphrase of our second fundamental. The techniques necessary to observing this principle are deceptively simple because they involve a single idea, but a complex set of muscle behaviors. If improper techniques are employed in the early stages of the learning process, movement patterns can be established that are detrimental to good performance. These bad habits, once acquired, are difficult to erase and make the learning of good habits immeasurably more difficult.

The most common bad habit is some form of unnecessary or undesirable motion. If you watch a good moving-target shooter, you'll see nothing flashy or showy in his performance. He appears to function with the minimum possible movement, and this is in fact heavily responsible for his success. No movement is wasted. Every movement is functional. His efforts have the appearance of elegance, a term we have used before in a different context. If elegance is a simplicity that underlies an apparent complexity, the successful moving-target shooter makes elegance visible in the economy and simplicity of his movements. The same elegance is apparent in all higher-level athletic performances.

To prevent unintentional learning of unnecessary or undesirable movements, we recommend that five stages be followed in learning moving-target marksmanship. All involve the acquisition of motor skills, that is, skills of muscle movement. Motor skills are not learned in a single practice session. For reasons that are not entirely clear, the optimal method of learning motor skills is to practice for a reasonable period once a day as long as desired. Following this pattern of practice is important and we cannot overemphasize its value.

The method outlined below is designed to enable skill acquisition to take place in a logical sequence. Each stage of the process should be mastered before you move on to the next stage. The first four stages are conducted with an *unloaded* gun.

Stage 1. Consists of learning to swing the gun smoothly. No target is necessary. Simply bring the gun into aiming position and practice swinging it smoothly and steadily at an imaginary target. Practice until you become thoroughly familiar with the feel of the movements and have acquired complete control of the muscles involved. A few minutes a day over a period of several days should allow time for you to develop good body awareness and for your muscles to "learn" their roles.

Stage 2. Consists of adding trigger pull to your swinging motion. Learn to pull the trigger smoothly without disturbing your swing or follow-through. Practice this a few minutes a day over a period of several days.

Stage 3. Consists of practice in tracking actual targets, but without a trigger pull. An economical way of doing this is to practice on targets other people are actually shooting at. At this stage you will find that you have to learn a new set of skills. In stages 1 and 2 you learned basic movements; in this stage, you learn timing and pace in order to track the target smoothly and steadily, without jerkiness or changes in rate of motion. This is a crucial step, for it involves developing complex and finely-tuned motor skills, and it is crucial that you master timing and pace before moving to the next stage. A few people can complete this stage in two or three practice sessions. Most people will require several more sessions.

Stage 4. Consists of integrating trigger pull into your swing and follow-through on actual targets. Again, the gun should be empty; you will be dry-firing. Do not be concerned at this stage that you're uncertain of the correct amount of lead to give to the target. Just use what you think is the correct lead and practice dry-firing until you can swing with the target, break the trigger, and follow through in a single smooth, flowing movement.

Stage 5. Consists of actual firing at the target. By this stage, if you have mastered the motor skills, there is only one thing to learn—the correct lead. Once you've found that, you can proceed to practice with the assurance that you have no bad habits—no uncoordinated movements, no unnecessary movements, no jerkiness—just a smooth elegance of motion. You will not be a master marksman, of course; there will be other things you will have to learn. But you'll be off to a good start, free of bad habits that might hamper your future development.

Whenever problems arise after you complete this stage, conduct a review of all five stages. If you're like most people, the review will enable you to isolate the problem, correct it, and bring your performance back to standard again almost immediately.

Now let's summarize.

Moving-target marksmanship is based upon the same two fundamentals that underlie stationary-target marksmanship. All the principles listed at the end of Chapter 2 should be employed where applicable. Only two additional principles are involved in moving-target marksmanship.

Principle 11. In tracking the target, the entire upper torso should pivot above the hips.

Principle 12. In tracking the target, gun motion should be smooth and steady until the completion of recoil.

Principle 12 is best learned in five stages. When a proficient shooter develops difficulties, a review of these five stages will often enable him to identify and correct the problem.

4
Vision in Shooting

You probably know Mark Twain's irreverent statement about the man who saw as through a glass eye, darkly.

Most of us know individuals who acquire this affliction whenever they pick up a gun. But did you know that even the sharpest human eye can be tricked by illusions, mirages, and ghosts? That these things exist, not only in association with legends, magic, and the supernatural, but in the scientific world of light waves, optical principles, sectional air densities, and visual chemistry? And that your own vision has undoubtedly been tricked by these things, and you didn't even know it?

We're accustomed to thinking of vision as a reliable way of sensing the world. We believe that if we see a thing, then it is what it appears to be, and it's where it appears to be. This belief is serviceable enough in most everyday circumstances and we are seldom called upon to question it. In shooting, however, we're forced to use our eyes in a much more critical and demanding way, and the tricks and errors of vision that have no effect in ordinary activities suddenly become extremely important. If we wish to be good shooters, we must re-evaluate our accustomed way of thinking about vision, as well as some widely accepted ways of thinking about sighting.

First, let's review some basic concepts. Everyone knows that vision is really a response to light waves reflecting or emanating from an object in space. We know that light waves travel in a straight line, enter the eye through the pupil, and eventually strike the retina, a light-sensitive mosaic of cells at the back of the eye. We know that the light waves are brought into focus on the retina by a variable lens which is located in front of the eye. The lens, by changing shape, can selectively focus light coming from objects at varying distances from the eye all the way from very close (6 to 8 inches) to very distant (a star). This all seems very straightforward and predictable, and for the most part it is. However, it is the exceptions that prove so interesting to the shooter.

If we examine certain of the assumptions in the previous paragraph, we find that they can be misleading. For one thing, light travels in a straight line only in a vacuum or in a transmitting medium of uniform density.* When light passes from a medium of one density into a medium of another density, the light rays are bent, or refracted. This explains why a straight rod thrust into a body of water appears bent.

The transmitting medium shooters are concerned with, of course, is air, a colorless, odorless gas. But gas is a state of matter; and like all states of matter it is subject to expansion with heat and to contraction with loss of heat. When very hot air comes into contact with very cold air, a boundary is created between two appreciably different air densities. The differences in air densities in a light path are called *sectional air densities* and occur quite commonly in nature. When the differences are extreme, alterations in light paths may also be extreme.

You have probably experienced one extreme effect of sectional air densities while driving along a highway on a hot, sunlit day. Under certain conditions, you can look far ahead on the road and see what appears to be a lake or a body of water on the highway. Yet when you approach that part of the road the lake disappears, an obvious illusion.

The explanation is quite simple. The "lake" is actually a portion of the sky reflected by an extremely hot layer of air over the road. The density of this layer of super-heated air is so much less than the cooler air above that nearly vertical

*This book omits the implications of Einsteinian relativity. For all practical purposes, shooting is governed by the laws of Newtonian physics.

light rays coming from the sky are bent or reflected in a roughly horizontal direction.

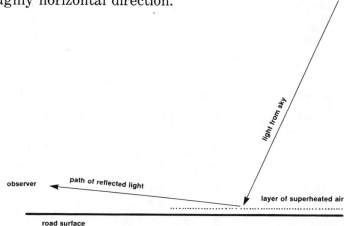

More complex illusions occur where extreme sectional air densities occur high in the atmosphere. One famous instance occurs in the Mediterranean region where the image of a city sometimes appears in the sky. The diagram illustrates distances great enough to include the curvature of the earth.

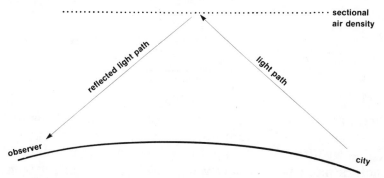

A still more complex illusion is often reported in the Sahara, where oases appear in the medium distance, only to vanish as a traveller approaches. In this case the light path is twice refracted by two separate sectional air densities:

A variation of this effect can occur when we look at a

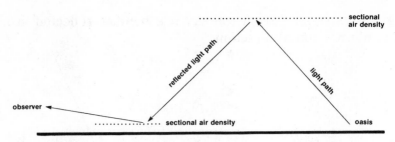

target object, especially one some distance removed from us on a hot, sunlit day. Variations in the heat-absorbing quality of the ground-surface between us and the target will create different sectional air densities. In these cases, light rays coming from the target may approach us by an indirect route, creating a displaced image some distance removed from the actual target. Since all the light reaching us from the target follows the same indirect path, the illusion is perfect: the displaced image of the target is the only image we can detect. A shot perfectly centered in the displaced target image may miss the actual target completely. The diagram illustrates.

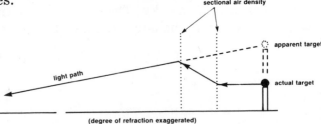

Displacement illusions are most pronounced at long distances, and decrease proportionately as the target distance decreases. Pistol and shotgun shooters, for example, are not frequently affected by them to any extreme degree, but rifle shooters must be constantly watchful for this effect whenever direct sunlight is heating the earth's surface. The effect is appreciable at distances even as close as 50 meters.

The best way to detect the existence of sectional air densities between you and a target is by looking through a spotting scope focused just short of the target. The displacement effect will be visible as a wavering or shimmering movement of the air, often called "mirage" by shooters. If there are no wind currents, the shimmering will appear as a vertical boiling motion, and the displaced image will appear above the actual target. If a wind is blowing from the side, the shimmering motion will seem to flow with the wind and the target image will be displaced in the direction of the flow. A wind blowing from left to right, for example, will cause the image to appear to the right of the actual target.

Since the displacement effect is infinitely variable, there is no simple formula for sight adjustments to compensate for it. Experience with reading the shimmering air through a spotting scope, however, will enable more astute shooters to make very accurate estimates of correct sight adjustments as necessary on a particular range on a particular day. An alternative is to leave sight adjustments unchanged and to displace the aim-point on the target, by using "Kentucky windage," a procedure that many people may find preferable, especially when wind conditions are variable.

The eye

So we must sometimes be concerned that light travelling to the eye can be misleading. Now let's look at problems arising from the way the eye itself responds to light.

We said earlier that light enters the eye through a pupil and passes to the back of the eye where it strikes the retina, a mosaic of light-sensitive cells. These cells are of two types, rods and cones, but essentially all of them respond to light in the same way.

The light striking the cells causes a chemical change within the cells, and this change stimulates electrical and chemical impulses that travel along neural fibers to the brain. The brain somehow assembles the impulses from millions of cells, and the result is vision.

The key to another troublesome vision problem lies in the nature of the chemical changes that occur in the retinal cells.

The chemistry involved obviously must regenerate itself constantly, which it does in normal situations if the image on the retina shifts or changes frequently. However, if a constant, unchanging image falls on the retina, the chemical process in the cells becomes fatigued; consequently, when the eye is shifted and the retinal image changes, a residual or "ghost" image is retained in the cells.

The problem is too complex to illustrate in all of its ramifications, but a simple experiment can give us a basic grasp of the problem. Using the diagram, stare fixedly at the center of the ringed target for 30 seconds. Then shift to the simple target and stare at its center. Soon after you shift to the simple target, a negative or white residual image of the ringed target will appear to hover on the simple target.

This illustrates the principle of retinal fatigue, but is not, as we've said, an adequate explanation of a rather complex phenomenon. Other complications can occur which are beyond the scope of this discussion. Our point, however, is that if you develop the habit of staring fixedly at a sight picture, you can introduce misleading vision problems related to retinal fatigue.

The way to avoid these problems is by constantly darting the eye around the sight picture instead of staring at a fixed point. Simple enough, and it can save you a lot of grief.

A third problem with vision has to do with how the eyes focus, and to demonstrate some concepts here we'll ask you to perform some simple experiments. The purpose of our first experiment is to demonstrate the principle of selective focus. It won't reveal anything you don't already know, but it will establish a baseline for clear discussion.

Experiment 7. Hold one finger about 10 inches in front of the eye you aim with and close the other eye. Sight across the top of your finger at an object at least several feet away, or even further. You will note that as you focus on the distant object, your finger appears blurred; and that as you focus on your finger, the distant object appears blurred.

Now extend your arm and repeat the process with your finger as far from your eye as you can get it. You should notice that the blurring effect diminishes noticeably, but not altogether.

What this simple experiment demonstrates is the common knowledge that the unaided eye cannot focus on near and far objects at the same time. Focus, in other words, is selective in terms of distance. However, when you moved your hand away from your face, you saw that the blurring was diminished, which indicates that there is a "depth" to the focal field. We might state the principle this way: at any selected focal point, objects within a short distance on the near and far sides of the focal point are also in focus. The depth of the focal field is increased when we focus on distant objects, and contracts when we focus on near objects.

Now let's apply this concept to an ordinary metallic rifle sight system (often called "iron sights") and we'll see immediately that it is extremely important. If you focus on the rear sight, the front sight will be somewhat blurred and the distant target may become indistinguishable from the background. Focus on the distant target, and the rear sight becomes an indistinguishable blur. Later we'll give solutions to this problem in separate discussions of mechanical sights for handguns, shotguns, and rifles. For now, let's examine a simple alternative to metallic sights.

The most effective solution to the selective focus problem is an optical sight system. The most familiar example is a telescope with crosshairs. However, the word telescope is associated with magnification, which is really not our concern here. An optical sight system may in fact have positive or negative magnification, or none at all.

The value of an optical system is that it can introduce an aiming device—crosshairs, a dot, a post, or whatever—into the same focal plane as the distant target. Blurring of the target or the sight system is thus completely eliminated.

Optical sight systems are available for pistols, shotguns, and rifles. Those for pistols and shotguns usually have neutral or very low magnification powers such as 1X or 1.5X. Rifle scopes range in power from 1X up to 40X, the most useful being 3X to 9X for hunting and 10X to 20X for target and varmint shooting. Variable-power models are also available, as are many other features such as illuminated reticles, rangefinding mechanisms, etc.

Magnification in an optical system is often desirable, but for practical use there is an upper limit to usable power. A magnifying system enlarges the target image, but equally enlarges any apparent movement of the gun while aiming. At high powers of magnification, the most minute gun movements cause the target to appear to zip and dart around the field of view like a flying bat pursuing insects. The amplified visual stimuli thus created, seriously disturb eye-hand coordination and can destroy even the best shooter's ability to place the shot accurately.

Among the more exotic new optical sight systems, one involves light-intensification capabilities for night use; and another employs a laser beam to project a small pencil of light onto the target. These systems are illegal for hunting and are too expensive and cumbersome for civilian target use, but undoubtedly have far-reaching military and law-enforcement applications.

Let's return now to the problems associated with metallic or iron sights. First we'll do two more simple experiments to establish basic concepts, then we'll discuss some basic principles, and finally we'll move to separate discussions for handguns, shotguns, and rifles.

Experiment 8. For this experiment you'll need a 3 x 5 card or piece of paper in which you've punched a pinhole about $\frac{1}{16}$th inch in diameter.

Repeat the exercise you performed in the previous experiment, sighting over your finger held about 10 inches from your face at a distant object. Now repeat again, this time looking through the pinhole held close in front of your eye. You should notice that as you look through the pinhole, the degree of blurring is considerably lessened—not removed, but lessened to the extent that you can simultaneously see both objects with much improved clarity.

This demonstrates a useful principle: depth of focus can be increased by looking through a small aperture placed close to the eye. We'll label this *enhanced depth of focus.*

The cause of this phenomenon is found in the divergence of light rays travelling from an object, but we need not concern ourselves with a full explanation here. Simply remember the principle, as it will be introduced into later discussions.

Experiment 9. Our purpose in this experiment is to illustrate two important differences between monocular and binocular vision. Hold up one finger a few inches in front of your face and sight over it at a distant object, but this time keep both eyes open. You should notice immediately that when you focus on a distant object, you see a double image of your finger; and when you focus on your finger, you see a double image of the target object. We'll label this *binocular double imagery.*

Now notice something else. As you focus on the distant object, one of the double finger images may seem more sharply defined than the other. You may not see this difference, in which case both your eyes are of about equal strength. But most people have a dominant eye which produces a stronger image than the other. You can tell which eye is dominant simply by shutting one eye: the stronger image will remain when the dominant eye remains open. We'll label this the *dominant eye image,* and both this and the *double imagery* concepts will recur in later discussions.

We have now defined a number of basic terms which are necessary to a discussion of using metallic sights: selective focus, depth of focus, enhanced depth of focus, double imagery, dominant eye, sight picture, sight alignment, and sight calibration. If you're sure what each of these terms means, fine—read on. If not, review the previous discussion until you feel comfortable with all the terms.

We turn now to a discussion of the three categories of firearms.

Shotgunning

Shotguns are not precision weapons in the same sense as rifles: they fire an expanding pattern of pellets instead of a single bullet, and they are designed primarily for moving targets at relatively close ranges. These characteristics require a sight system of only moderate precision, but one that can be used with speed and quickness. Thus the most common sight system consists of a bead front sight and a simple sighting ramp or rib over the receiver to provide basic alignment.

There are some exceptions. A few shotguns designed to fire rifled slugs, and drilling guns (combination rifle/shotguns) are equipped with rifle sights. For a discussion of this type of sight system, refer to the riflery section of this chapter.

The basic sighting problem with a shotgun is achieving a consistent sight alignment while tracking a moving target. Consistency is largely a matter of positioning the gun to the shoulder, the cheek to the stock, and the eye to the gun in the same way each time. This insures consistency not only of sighting, but of recoil as well.

The best assurance of consistency is a gun that fits you individually. It should fall easily into place against the shoulder and point naturally and comfortably at the target. Your cheek should rest comfortably against the stock and the bead sight should center naturally in the rear sighting ramp. If you must strain arms, shoulder, or neck to aim the gun, it doesn't fit you. Seek another gun with a different combination of stock length, drop, and comb until you find the one that's right for you. You'll recognize it when you find it. As you look for the right gun, be sure to wear the same clothes you'll be wearing when you actually shoot; a single heavy layer of clothing can significantly alter a gun's fit.

To maintain consistency, learn to track a moving target by pivoting your upper torso from the hips. If you track by swinging from your shoulders, you change the gun's relationship to both your shoulder and your cheek, affecting recoil and sighting.

When you're using a shotgun against a moving target, you should probably keep both eyes open and focus on the target, for it is with binocular vision that we are best able to judge the speed and direction of a moving object. This of course produces double imagery of the front sight.

This can create a problem if you're a right-handed shooter and have a dominant left eye, or vice-versa. In this case you're likely to draw a bead on your target with the wrong eye, a situation guaranteed to produce a miss. If your dominant eye is the "wrong" eye, you might be advised to close that eye when shooting, or train yourself to sight with the correct eye.

A common failure for some shooters is to draw a bead on a rapidly-moving target without lowering the head to place the cheek on the stock. This also produces a miss, and if combined with a dominant "wrong" eye, the results are hopeless.

To summarize:

1. Seek consistency in placing the buttplate against the shoulder.

2. Seek consistency in placing the cheek against the stock, and the eye to the gun.

3. Track with both eyes open and focused on the target.

4. Aim with the correct eye; if the wrong eye is dominant, close it or learn to sight with the correct eye.

If you follow these principles and are still missing targets, the problem may be your sight picture, i.e., the amount of lead you're taking on the moving target. Experiment with different leads and different ways of achieving leads until you find one that suits your particular target.

And don't forget that a shotgun pattern, even though it produces an expanding cone of fire, nevertheless follows a downward curving trajectory that is much shorter and steeper than the trajectory of a typical rifle or pistol bullet. The trajectory curve will vary widely with pellet size and powder charge. Failure to take shotgun trajectories into consideration undoubtedly accounts for many of the "mysterious" misses that occur in shotgunning.

Handgunning

In some military and law-enforcement situations, the necessity to shoot quickly and at close quarters makes visual aiming unnecessary or even undesirable. A soldier or policeman may then shoot "from the hip," relying on his natural pointing instincts. In a face-to-face shoot-out situation, the results often hinge on which combatant is the faster. An interesting and well-informed book on this subject is Bill Jordan's "No Second Place Winner" (available from the NRA Book Service).

In less extraordinary circumstances, however, or at any great distance under any circumstances, it is almost always preferable to shoot a handgun with careful aim.

A handgun is the most difficult kind of gun to shoot accurately for several reasons. One is that the support system provided by the human body to a handgun is of almost ramshackle construction compared to the support given to a rifle.

The gun is gripped solely by the hand, which is connected to a pivoting wrist joint, a hinged elbow joint, and a ball-and-socket shoulder joint. This alone accounts for much of the difficulty in pistol shooting.

But there are other problems as well. One is that a handgun's extremely short barrel cannot produce the same precision of bullet spin and trajectory as can a longer rifle barrel. Related to this is that the handgun's short and therefore lightweight barrel lacks the inertial stability of a heavy rifle barrel—it can drift off target much more rapidly. And finally, the short barrel produces an extraordinarily short sight radius (distance between front and rear sights) which is inherently less precise than the longer sight radius of a rifle.

When you think about it, it's a wonder anybody ever hits anything with a pistol. To be sure, the standards of accuracy in pistol shooting are light years away from those in precision rifle shooting. But this in no way diminishes the skills of expert handgun shooters, who in their field are just as skillful as expert rifle shooters are in theirs. It's an instance of comparing apples to oranges.

The most important element in handgun aiming is to position the eye in relation to the gun in the same way each time. The next most important thing is sight alignment. The extremely short sight radius makes even the tiniest alignment error throw the bullet well away from the aim-point at normal shooting distances. Therefore the aiming eye should be focused on the sights, not on the target. Since the gun is held at arm's length, and the sight radius is normally measured in inches, depth of focus is usually great enough to allow a clear image of front and rear sights simultaneously.

Keeping both eyes open creates multiple double imagery problems. Focusing on the front sight, for example, creates double imagery not only of the target, but of the rear sight as well. It is therefore highly desirable to close the non-aiming eye. Some shooters prefer to block the non-aiming eye by wearing shooting glasses with tape over one lens. A variation is to attach flip-down sunglasses to the shooting glasses, with one of the flip-down lenses taped; the other can be removed if desired.

Enhanced depth of focus can be achieved by punching a small hole in a piece of tape and placing it on the glass lens in front of the aiming eye. Some experimentation is necessary to find the proper placement of the aperture. If this is done with prescription glasses, the aperture should be on or close to the optical center of the lens in order to retain its corrective properties.

With focus on the sight system, the target will appear blurred. Even with enhanced depth of focus achieved with a small aperture placed in front of the aiming eye, this blurring will be quite noticeable. Beginners find the blurring to be bothersome and distracting. Experience and training, however, enable you to achieve very good sight pictures on the blurred target and truly remarkable aiming accuracy can be attained through training and practice.

Anyone completely unable to adjust to target blurring might consider visiting an ophthalmologist and ordering a pair of glasses with a small plus lens ground into or cemented onto the lens in front of the aiming eye. This is a costly step, however, and does not eliminate, but only reduces, the degree of blurring. It should not be necessary except in extreme cases.

Riflery

A fine rifle matched with the proper ammo may have an almost incredible consistency. The most consistent guns when fired from a cradle can produce shot groups of less than one inch at 300 meters.

While this degree of consistency is rare, many commercially manufactured target guns can group within a 2- to 6-inch circle at this distance when matched with the right ammunition. Of course, guns that are less well-made cannot be expected to have anywhere near this kind of consistency.

Optical sight systems (telescopes) are ideally suited for rifles for several obvious reasons. Their application was discussed earlier in this chapter. There are occasions, however, when a telescope is undesirable, or forbidden by the rules of competition.

For various reasons, many hunters choose metallic sights. In most cases, they will use a notched rear sight and a blade front sight. The open rear sight (as opposed to an aperture sight) allows the eye to maintain continuous focus on game while mounting the gun, an advantage when game is difficult to spot in its surroundings or difficult to track because it is moving.

Whether you keep one or both eyes open with these sights is largely a matter of individual preference, but if both eyes are kept open, you must make sure that you're not being confused by double imagery—either of rear sight, front sight, or target.

Because sight alignment is the more critical part of the sight picture even with a rifle, focus should be on the front sight, or perhaps a bit forward or behind it. In practice, focus will probably move from rear sight to front sight to the target and then back to the front sight as the shot is squeezed off. During the squeeze, concentration should be on maintaining sight alignment within the over-all sight picture.

Target sights for riflery

Target shooting, especially regulation competition shooting, imposes more stringent demands. There is usually no advantage to be gained from open sights, and the requirement for easily variable and precisely adjustable sights has led to the development of an aperture system.

Target sights are usually detachable. In the most common designs, both front and rear sights are attached by sliding the sights onto grooved mounting blocks and tightening with thumb screws. The mounting block for the rear sight is sometimes built into the receiver. In any case, the rear mounting block is usually long enough to allow the sight to be moved backward and forward a distance of several inches.

The rear sight. The rear sight should affix firmly to the mounting block and should have precise micrometer click adjustments on both horizontal and vertical axes. Looseness in the mount or adjustment mechanisms can seriously affect accuracy.

The rear aperture should be variable in size. This can be accomplished by changing inserts, but a more convenient design is a single insert with an iris diaphragm that can be varied by simply turning an adjustment ring.

The rear sight should be mounted close to the eye, but not so close that recoil causes it to slam into the brow. The distance between the rear sight and the eye is called *eye relief*, and the preferred distance varies from shooter to shooter and from position to position. In smallbore competition, eye relief for some shooters in the prone position is less than an inch; in the standing position it may be three to seven inches.

This rear aperture target sight has micrometer adjustments in both the horizontal and vertical axes. A variable iris diaphragm allows easy adjustment of aperture size.

Generally, eye relief falls within these ranges for all shooters and positions.

The closer the rear sight is to the eye, the smaller the rear aperture that can be used, and the greater the enhancement of depth of focus. It should be noted, however, that below a certain minimum size, and aperture will interfere with the light waves passing through it by a complex phenomenon called diffraction. Diffraction seriously affects clarity of vision and you can usually detect its presence. Turn the adjustment ring to reduce the size of the aperture; at some point, the clarity of the image seen through the aperture will noticeably diminish. At this point you have passed the diffraction threshold, and should open the aperture at least one or two clicks in order to insure that the phenomenon does not interfere with your vision.

Another consideration, however, is the pattern the rear aperture forms with the front sight hood. Generally, you will want the rear aperture to appear about 1½ times the diameter of the front sight hood. You may want it slightly larger or smaller than this, but experience shows this to be the most satisfactory and widely used formula. The ideal rear aperture size, then, is one that provides no diffraction interfer-

Many marksmen prefer to hold both eyes open but to block vision in the non-aiming eye by attaching a simple screen to the rear sight.

ence, good depth enhancement, and an apparent diameter about 1½ times that of the front hood. Often, a compromise must be made between the last two considerations. Diffraction interference is never acceptable.

The front sight. The front sight normally consists of a tube-like hood which can accept interchangeable inserts. In many types of competition, the length and size of the hood are subject to regulations. (Consult your rulebook.) Metal inserts—usually apertures, sometimes posts—are traditional. Transparent plastic discs of various colors, with a black outline surrounding the aperture, are also popular.

Aperture inserts should appear to be about 1½ times the diameter of the bull. Again, you may prefer a slightly smaller

Some variation is possible in front aperture size. Illustrated here are about the maximum and minimum useful sizes in relation to the apparent diameter of the bull. If the front aperture is too large or too small, the advantages of the aperture system are lost.

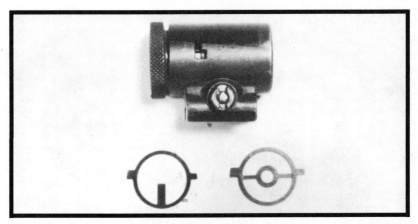

**This front sight hood accepts interchangeable inserts. Shown
are metal post and aperture inserts.**

or larger aperture, but this is the generally acceptable formula.

Post inserts are used by a few people, but there is actually
a very good reason not to use a post. The post provides only
a very small image to pattern with the bull, and this places
a greater burden upon the resolving power of the eye. If a
post is used, its width should appear identical to the diameter
of the bull, and it should approach the bull from 6 o'clock. It
may either touch the bottom boundary of the bull, or a thin
line of white may be maintained between the top of the post
and the bull. The post should never pattern by cutting into
the bull, because human visual acuity is not capable of judging pattern consistency in this configuration. A few shooters
prefer to use post sights in the standing position and aperture sights in other positions.

The desired sight pictures with target sights have been
illustrated in the photos, using the formula of about 1½
diameter measurements. Note the ease of maintaining sight
alignment using the pattern of concentric circles. The correct
post sight pattern is also illustrated.

The rear aperture should appear to be about 1½ times the diameter of the front sight hood, as shown here.

Two problems with aperture sights

There are two common problems with aperture sights. One is that the bull may appear to flatten on one side. This is caused by imperfect centering of the eye behind the rear aperture. You can illustrate this very simply by looking through your aperture sights and moving your head to the right: the left side of the bull will appear to flatten or fade. The solution, of course, is merely to adjust head position.

The other common problem is that under certain light conditions, a given aperture size will cause the bull to lose contrast and appear an indistinct gray. Sometimes the problem can be solved by varying the size of the rear aperture. If this does not work, then you'll need to vary the front aperture.

You may never have this problem. Some people never do. But if you do, note what light change produces the effect (such as a change from overcast to direct sunlight, from front to back lighting, etc.) and also whether your solution is to increase or decrease your normal aperture sizes. Memorizing the solution will save you valuable time in competitive events.

Eye care

Please wear protective shooting glasses, no matter what kind of gun you use. Protective lenses (as well as ear protectors) are now required in most competitive events. Bits of debris can ricochet back into the eyes from the discharge of a gun, and a ruptured cartridge-case or barrel can cause instant blindness.

Protective glasses are offered by several manufacturers. The lenses are tempered to withstand the impact of a ¾ inch steel ball dropped from a height of 50 inches. They are relatively inexpensive and well worth the investment.

Shooting glasses come in clear, tinted, and photochrome lenses. Many shooters like to use gray or green lenses in bright light, but they are not essential. Neither are amber lenses, which some individuals say increase target contrast on overcast or foggy days. This effect may be noticed by some people, but most cannot detect any appreciable advantage in amber lenses.

Corrective lenses are used with complete satisfaction by a great proportion of shooters. Contact lenses are unquestionably the most convenient form. If normal spectacles are used, the eye should sight through the center of the lens to benefit fully from its corrective power. This is very difficult in the prone position, and some shooters have special lenses especially ground with the optical center in the line of vision when the head is in the prone shooting position. A few shooters have special glasses made up for all positions. A complete set of glasses is expensive, but appears to work well. You will be wise to have such glasses prescribed by an ophthalmologist who is familiar with shooting and, even better, who will take measurements for the glasses while you are actually in your shooting positions, with your gun.

A much less expensive alternative is to buy shooting glasses with adjustable frames that allow you to bring the optical center of the lens into proper relationship to your eye in all three shooting positions. Only a single lens need be ground, and tinted lenses can be interchanged with clear ones if you desire. Adjustable-frame shooting spectacles are currently manufactured only in Europe, but are available from various gun dealers such as Freeland.

You should bear in mind that your own eyes are unique and differ from other people's eyes as much as your face differs from their faces. The sight adjustments and aperture sizes that are right for someone else may be completely wrong for you, and vice-versa. Don't let someone else's preferences or opinions convince you that because you do not like the eye relief or aperture sizes he uses, then there must be something wrong with your own vision.

If you have not had your eyes examined by an ophthalmologist (as opposed to an optometrist) in several years, you should probably do so. If you have eye problems or need to use corrective lenses, he can tell you and even help you design special shooting glasses if you want them. Then, when you know your own vision is sound and healthy, design and use the sight system that's right, and works for you.

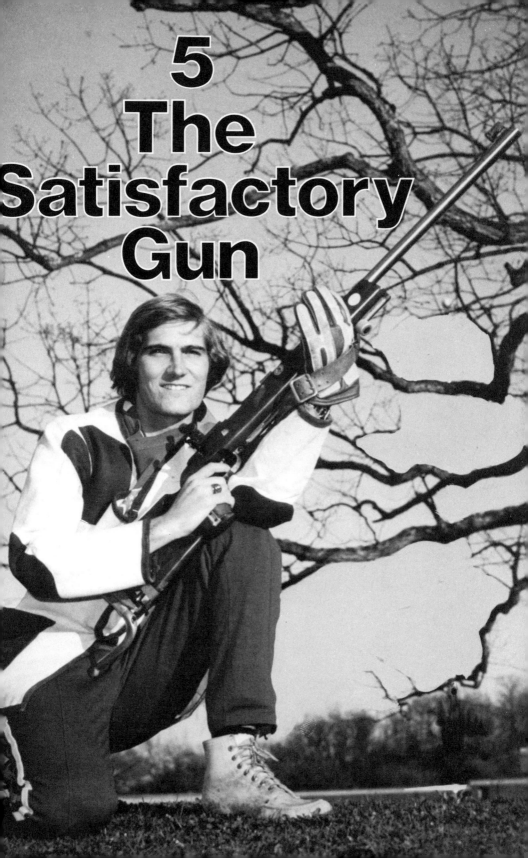

5
The Satisfactory Gun

Virtually everyone who shoots is concerned about firearm quality. You naturally want a gun that has consistency and mechanical reliability. Confidence in your gun is in fact very important, because if you're worrying about your gun, your mind's not devoted to your own performance, and this can wreck your ability to shoot accurately.

Our view is that you should buy a high-quality gun—one that is right for you and is reliable and consistent—so you can have confidence in it and concentrate on honing your own performance skills. Except for routine maintenance and periodic testing, don't concern yourself about equipment. Too many beginning shooters never show progress because they keep searching for a better gun instead of working on their own performance. This is equivalent to a beginning violinist believing that he could instantly become a concert artist if he could only acquire a Stradivarius. The secret to success does not lie in the gun or violin, but in the performer.

In this chapter we're going to be concerned about selecting a gun and testing it for consistency, or its ability to fire small groups. But bear in mind that consistency is not the only important quality of a gun. Just as important is how well the gun fits you, how it feels when you're aiming and firing. A gun that feels awkward or unsuited to you, even though it possesses remarkable consistency, may not allow you to achieve nearly the accuracy you could get with a less consistent gun that fits you perfectly. Gun consistency is important and cannot be ignored; but gun consistency alone will not make you a good marksman.

Before buying a gun, then, look for the proper fit even before testing it for consistency. Proper fit is partly physical, partly psychological.

Physically, the gun should have the proper feel in your

hands. It should give the impression of a correct weight and balance; it should fit the contours of your body; and it should point naturally and comfortably at the target when you aim.

But a gun should also fit you psychologically, and you may not be able to determine this until you've fired it a few times. Any number of features may come into play here. Do you feel that the gun is too small, too light, too heavy, too expensive, too inexpensive? Is it too high-powered, so that you come to dread the recoil or the report? Is there something about the gun that you simply do not like? If nagging doubts of this type arise with a gun, then it doesn't fit you psychologically and it's not likely that you'll ever reach your full potential with it. Look for another gun that's "right."

Let's turn now to the question of what makes a gun consistent, or able to fire tight groups. This is, of course, a kind of million dollar question, and literally volumes have been devoted to answering it. If you're interested in gunsmithing, accurizing, or ballistic engineering, you might want to read some of the many books on the subject.

We're going to assume, however, that you're not interested in becoming a gun mechanic, but that you are interested in buying and using a gun you can have confidence in. If you're thoughtful about your selections, you can purchase over-the-counter items that will give you a completely solid foundation. You may find, in fact, that these items are all you will ever need. If you progress to high-level competitive marksmanship, you may opt to customize your equipment or to buy original custom equipment produced by small, private manufacturers of high-quality gun parts.

But whatever route you choose, gun consistency results from two basic functions: the quality of design and manufacture of the gun itself; and ammunition that is matched to that particular, individual gun.

To determine which is the best quality gun currently on the market, find out what the best shooters are using. It helps if you know an advanced marksman personally, but you don't have to. The advertisements in magazines dealing with shooting sports, as well as gun and shooting articles in those magazines, will provide you with up-to-date information. You can also get information by writing to the gun editors of these magazines, describing in detail what you want and need, and asking for a reply. If the magazine is a reputable one, you should get a reliable answer. Other sources of information are knowledgeable friends; books; gun dealers; local gun clubs; and civilian, police, and military shooting teams.

In general, we recommend buying the best quality gun you can afford. Be sure you're paying for mechanical quality, however, instead of fancy ornamentation. A lot of gold and silver inlay and unique stock designs may look nice, but they don't improve your marksmanship.

After you've narrowed your choices to a reasonable number of brand-names and models, visit a reputable dealer and actually handle the guns to get a feel for them. Chances are you'll quickly acquire a preference for one or two of the models. Then, if it's at all possible, arrange to test-fire the guns before you make a purchase. Many dealers will arrange for a test on their own private firing ranges or at a nearby gun-club range, and may charge a fee for this service. Or they may allow you to purchase the gun with the option of returning it within a specified time, in which case you can arrange your own test. Unless you know the dealer well, ask for this agreement in writing.

You can accomplish two things during a test-firing. First, you can determine whether or not the gun fits you psychologically—whether you actually enjoy firing it. And second, you can test the gun's consistency. (In some cases, with better firearms, consistency will have been tested before the gun leaves the factory, and you will be supplied with a test-group target bearing the gun's serial number.)

The purest test for consistency, of course, is to fire the gun from a vise, cradle, or other mechanical device that eliminates shooter error. However, this procedure is not readily available to most shooters, and, in addition, by itself does not indicate how well the gun is matched to you individually.

Moreover, you should never attempt to fire a gun from a vise or cradle you make up yourself unless you're equipped with special knowledge; otherwise you may damage the gun, yourself, or both.

Therefore, whether or not you have access to mechanical test devices, you should test-fire the gun personally. We recommend that you use a bench rest equipped with sandbags or similar supports, and that you test fire groups on paper targets at a reasonable distance. After firing each group, remove the target and write on it the kind of ammunition used and any other notes you wish to make. The target may be kept as a permanent record.

Before firing, check the gun to make sure the barrel is clear and the gun is in proper mechanical condition. If you do not understand completely how to operate the gun, ask or read about it so you can use it safely. And of course check downrange to make certain that nothing is in your line of fire that shouldn't be there.

Next, fire a few rounds through the gun to "clear the barrel" of lubricants or solvents that will affect the friction of the barrel against the bullets. You should follow this procedure every time you begin firing after the bore has been cleaned or oiled, for the lubricants will usually cause the first round or two to follow an abnormal trajectory.

Also consider this. Firing a gun heats the barrel and chamber, causing the metal to expand and change shape. This too will have an effect upon trajectory. If you expect to use your gun in matches that require long strings of shots, you will want to test the gun with a warmed-up barrel. On the other hand, if you expect to use the gun in hunting where you will normally fire only a single round through a cold barrel, you will want to test it with a cold barrel by letting it cool off between rounds.

Assume a comfortable, stable position at your bench rest. Arrange your equipment so that everything is conveniently within reach, and adjust your position so that you are aiming naturally and steadily at the target. You should always wear protective glasses and hearing protectors while test firing.

Now we're ready to discuss ammunition. When testing a gun for consistency, you will get more reliable results if you fire several different brands, loads, and lot-numbers of ammo. Do not mix these; fire at least two test groups with each brand, load, or lot number, and record the information on the target. Usually, one particular load will perform best in a particular gun. (A lot number is the number assigned to each "lot" or production-run of ammunition as it moves through the factory. The number is usually stamped or printed on the end-flaps of the packing carton or box. The runs vary from one another in differing degrees, but the effects on consistency will usually be noticeable and even significant in high-precision shooting.)

If you're an advanced shooter already involved in hand-loading ammunition, you'll be familiar with this kind of testing. Very slight variations in ammo components can appreciably affect group-size. If you are at this stage, you may want to test the gun using different hand-loads, and perhaps try to "build" a load for your particular gun. This is a superior way of fine-tuning the match between gun and ammo, and many advanced shooters, particularly in riflery, depend upon custom hand-loads for the best results. Shotgunners and handgunners find less need for this procedure.

Depending on your own requirements, factory loads may be entirely adequate for your needs. Only you can decide this. But you owe it to yourself, after investing in a fine gun, to determine which ammunition is best suited for it. We emphasize that this is a matter of individual guns. Two seemingly identical factory models of a gun may well perform best with two entirely different brands, loads, or lot numbers of ammo.

Let's look now at some considerations in testing and evaluating different types of guns.

Shotguns

A shotgun is normally used to throw a rather wide shot pattern, in which case there is no need to be concerned about pin-point consistency. The large pattern will usually exceed the target size by more than enough margin to make up for consistency errors in the gun.

There are two exceptions, however.

If the gun is used to fire rifled slugs, you will want it to have at least a reasonable consistency. What is reasonable? Well, when you consider that such a gun-ammo combination is designed for use on large, heavy game animals at close range, there is an acceptable margin. If the gun could fire a 12-inch group at 50 meters, the radius of error would be only 6 inches, and only 3 inches at 25 meters. That certainly seems adequate for body shots at most big-game animals at distances up to 25 meters.

Shotguns, especially semi-automatics, vary widely in slug-throwing consistency. The best bet is to test a gun before buying it by firing several groups, each with a different brand and/or load. One of the brands or loads will usually produce the smallest groups. There is no need to test-fire a shotgun from a cradle or other mechanical device.

The second situation where consistency is a factor in shot-gunning is when you're using a double barreled gun. Most finer guns are made well enough that both barrels throw shot-patterns (or slugs) at the same aim-point. Some doubles, however, have barrels that are not aimed at the same point, and this must be taken into account when you form a sight picture. You can be fairly assured that the aim-points, while different, remain in a fixed relationship to each other, and you can easily adjust your aim to accomodate the barrel you're firing. If you're interested in firing slugs in a double barrel, it will be worthwhile to test each barrel individually. In many cases, one will have better slug-throwing ability than the other.

Normally, test-firings of shotguns are not conducted to

determine consistency, but the patterns produced when the gun is used with various shot shells. This is a common sense procedure based on firing at spread sheets of newspaper or similar targets at some determined distance. Only one shell is fired at each target, and the diameter of the shot pattern is easily determined by a quick inspection. Different brands and loads of shells may produce different size patterns; but probably a stronger determiner is the choke of the barrel. Some shotgunners who need more versatility than is provided by a single fixed-choke barrel, have a reputable gunsmith alter the choke, buy interchangeable barrels or have variable-choke devices installed on their guns. The latter choice is less expensive and provides greater versatility. A large percentage of shotgunners, though, will have no need of either option if they are careful in making the right choke selection at the time of purchase.

Handguns

For our purposes in a book like this, handguns fall into two categories, but not the familiar ones of revolvers and semi-automatics. The categories we prefer are first, handguns designed for personal defense, and second, handguns designed for marksmanship accuracy. There is considerable overlapping in these categories, but the following general distinctions are useful.

Personal defense handguns are usually compact and short-barreled. They are designed to be worn in a holster and are built for speed and ease of handling. The better ones are rugged and reliable under a variety of conditions. The most common types are revolvers and semi-automatics.

Marksmanship handguns are often bulky, heavy, and long-barreled. They are not designed for normal holster wear and to be used effectively must be fired at a relatively slow, deliberate pace. Ruggedness takes second place to consistency in the design of these guns. The most common types are semi-automatics and single-shots.

These distinctions are obviously too broad to apply in every case, but they are nevertheless useful in forming expectations about the marksmanship potential of a handgun. A handgun designed for personal defense simply may not give you pin-point consistency at 20 meters, even when fired from a cradle under the best of conditions. It was not designed with high-level consistency as a first consideration. To be sure, many personal defense handguns do provide an admirable consistency, given handgun limitations, but even the better ones represent compromises with portability and ease of handling, which, after all, are perhaps the most desirable features of a personal defense handgun. Otherwise, one would choose a shotgun or rifle for personal defense.

This is not to say, of course, that personal defense handguns are unsuitable for marksmanship purposes. They are. It just means that you cannot, in fairness, expect a personal defense handgun to strike matches at ten paces. Large targets are the rule, and target distances are relatively short. At distances where a good bench-rest rifle would put every bullet through the same hole, a personal defense handgun fired from a bench rest might produce a shot group much larger in diameter and still be perfectly acceptable for its intended purpose. Larger targets allow for lesser consistency, and the skill of the marksman may be every bit as great as the skill of the best rifleman. Standards of accuracy are lower; standards of skill are not.

For greater consistency, you will want one of the heavier, bulkier target pistols. In many respects, these guns are "little rifles" because their triggers, chambers, and barrel designs often closely resemble rifle components. Though remarkably consistent, even the best cannot compete with rifles because they lack the rifle's inertial stability and consistency-producing barrel length.

The logical method of selecting a handgun is to decide what type you want—a personal defense weapon, a marksmanship weapon, or some compromise between the two—and then begin examining the various brands and models available. If you're fortunate enough to know a top-notch handgun shooter, you may be able to get not only up-to-date information on the best guns, but perhaps help in making a selection, and instruction as well.

In making a selection, consider not only how suitable the gun is to your purposes and how consistent it is, but also how well it fits you physically and psychologically. If the gun does not conform to your grip, feel balanced and "right" in your hand, and point naturally, you may never become proficient with it. Most over-the-counter guns are fitted with a grip designed to conform to the average hand, and remarkable improvements in the feel of a handgun can result from equipping it with custom grips. You might want to consider this if the gun is desirable in all other respects but doesn't fit your hand.

But there is also a unique psychological fit to a handgun. If you worry about the gun because it is the wrong caliber, poorly made, or unsuited to your needs, you won't be able to perform well with it. One of the more common errors is to buy an overpowered gun with excessive recoil and report. This will induce you to tense up and flinch when firing; the result is a disturbed aim and ultimately a psychological distaste for the weapon. Choose a gun that fits physically and psychologically and then you can concentrate fully on your own performance skills.

The purest test for consistency is to fire the gun from a armorer's cradle, but this is seldom practicable and, besides, does not indicate how the gun performs in your hand. For the same reason, you should not rely on someone else's tests of the gun. The final judgment of handgun accuracy must be derived from *your* results with it, and with handguns this is a highly individualized and personal matter.

Once you've chosen your gun, you may want to have it worked over by a competent gunsmith. Factory-model handguns can be customized for improved reliability, consistency, or both. The work can range from a simple tune-up to an almost complete rebuilding job. But use caution. Any gunsmith can claim he can do the work for you. If he's inexperienced you may just waste your money. A good gunsmith with a few years of experience, however, can often increase a gun's consistency and reliability, and also your accuracy with the gun, by improving its feel in your hand through better weight distribution, more comfortable grips, and superior sights and trigger.

If you're a competitive hangunner, you may want to develop hand-loaded ammunition, particularly with inflation prices soaring, generally speaking, factory loaded, center fire pistol ammunition is more accurate than the average shooter can load.

Rifles

In riflery the demands for consistency in a gun are much higher than in shotgunning or handgunning, but there is no single standard that can be applied to all rifles. Rifles are designed to meet different requirements. A military assault rifle, for example, is designed for reliability under adverse conditions, a high rate of fire, ease of operation and maintenance, and other features important to military use. Such a gun may produce a shot-group a couple of feet in diameter at 300 meters and still be acceptable for its purpose. On the other hand, a precision bench-rest rifle may be capable of 2-inch or smaller groups at 300 meters, but be so cumbersome, slow to use, and sensitive to environmental conditions that it would have little value for anything other than bench-rest use.

We'll concentrate on two categories of rifles—those for hunting, and those for target use. There is some overlap between the two (a long-range varmint rifle for instance), but generally it is best to select a gun designed specifically for one or the other purpose.

Your first consideration in selecting a hunting rifle should probably be ballistical characteristics. You want a caliber that is neither too powerful nor too light for the game you intend to hunt. You will usually find a range of calibers that fit your requirements, and you choose among them by weighing such factors as carrying weight, foot-pounds of impact energy, flatness of trajectory, range, susceptibility of the bullet to deflection by wind and small environmental objects, and even availability and price.

Once this issue is decided, you will probably do just as well to stick with a good over-the-counter hunting rifle by a reputable manufacturer. Custom built hunting rifles are fine for the enthusiast, but are really not necessary except in the most unusual circumstances. Choose a model that fits you well and feels right in your hands, and arrange to test-fire it. If possible, test-fire two different models, or even duplicates of the same model.

Run tests at the distances you expect to shoot at game, using as many different brands, loads, and lot-numbers of ammunition as you reasonably can. Keep careful records, and, if applicable, remember to let the gun barrel cool off between rounds. There is really no necessity to test a new hunting rifle in a cradle unless you're worried about extraordinarily high-precision consistency. A good test conducted from a bench-rest will be all you'll need.

The diameter of the shot groups will give a clear indication of your accuracy with the gun and a reasonable idea of the gun's consistency. How small should the shot groups be? A good means of judging is to consider the size of the vital areas of the game you'll be hunting. A vital area is not of pinpoint dimensions—it is a fairly large area usually centering over the heart, the brain, or the neck. The shot group sizes you're getting on your target are acceptable if they are equal to or smaller than the vital areas of your intended game. Smaller is better of course, especially when you consider that in hunting you may not have a rest as solid as a bench-rest table. But in normal circumstances, you should be able, by testing various gun and ammo combinations, to find a rifle that possesses more than adequate consistency for your needs.

Target rifles pose different kinds of considerations. Caliber selection is not much of an issue, especially in air-rifle and .22 rimfire events. There are also fairly clear caliber preferences for big-bore events because of the inherent ballistic superiority, availability, and cost of certain calibers and loads. These shift from time to time as advances are made in bullet design, and so your best bet is to find out what the better shooters are currently using. Again, you can usually determine this by reading the magazines devoted to shooting sports.

In air-rifle and rimfire categories, over-the-counter rifles are widely used by even the best world-class marksmen. If you're considering buying a rifle in these categories, we recommend that you test-fire several rifles with as many different varieties of target ammunition as you can find. If you find a gun-ammo combination that produces outstanding groups, stick with that combination and don't tamper with the gun in any way that would affect the bedding of the gun in the stock. If you find a gun that has acceptable consistency, but that you believe could be improved by glass-bedding, then you might consider this as an option after you purchase the gun. (Glass bedding is a process in which the stock is modified to accept viscous fiberglass. The gun is then bedded in the fiberglass, which hardens to form a theoretically perfect fit with the gun, thereby eliminating the effect of the stock upon the gun's inherent consistency. In practice, it works reasonably well, but is not foolproof.) Make sure the bedding is done expertly, preferably by someone with extensive experience.

If you're going to take this step, you might also consider going a bit further and using a stock made of an artificial material such as fiberglass that is less susceptible to warping in response to environmental conditions.

Big-bore target rifles are sometimes over-the-counter items, and there's no reason not to use such a gun if it possesses the required consistency. A majority of big-bore competition rifles, however, are the result of extensive custo-

The free-rifle, with its adjustable dimensions and heavy weight for inertial stability, is a favorite with target shooters.

mizing. A typical big-bore free-rifle, for example, might consist of an action produced by one manufacturer, a barrel produced by another, a trigger by another, and a glass-bedded stock perhaps made of artificial material. The ammunition might be hand-loaded for that particular rifle, and the cartridge cases may even be fire-formed in the chamber prior to loading, a meticulous practice available only to the hand-loader. It is almost redundant to say that big-bore target shooting is a highly individualized effort, with many people using unique components.

The standard for consistency among target rifles varies, but generally the gun that will form a group larger than the x-ring on the target is unacceptable for high level competition. For beginners or less serious competitors, a group that stays inside the 10-ring might be acceptable; but everyone wants a target rifle that will put bullet after bullet through the same hole. While this ideal is not absolutely attainable with current ballistics, it may be in the future with guns that fire a harmless laser beam against a target with electronic sensors. Laser guns, should they ever be adopted for competition, will eliminate ballistical errors and provide the truest test yet devised of human skill in marksmanship events.

Care of guns and ammunition

A fine gun is made up of many precision parts fashioned from costly metals. Dirt, grime, or rust will affect it adversely and eventually ruin it. Keep your gun clean and properly lubricated. The manufacturer's instructions will give you proper guidance, and good cleaning materials are readily available in gun stores. Form the habit of cleaning and lubricating your gun regularly after every use; after every exposure to dust, dirt, or water; and during prolonged storage. An old adage says, "if a dirty bore shoots well, a clean one will shoot better." Clean it often and well.

A gun should be stored and transported in a protective case. For travel, you should have a canvas or leather case as a minimum; a hard aluminum case with gasket seals and padded lining is even better. The gun should be protected from jolts, bumps, and pressure against the barrel (such as propping it in a corner), as the pressure that results can affect the trueness of the barrel, the bedding, the sights, the stock, or the inner mechanisms. Be careful of the gun when you handle it yourself, but be extra careful when you entrust it to a commercial carrier during moving or travel. Broken stocks are not unusual among commercially shipped guns.

Ammunition also needs protection from jolts, aging, and extreme changes in temperature and air pressure. Jolting can result in changes in seating, bullet shape, and cartridge shape. Any of these can affect performance. Aging can pro-

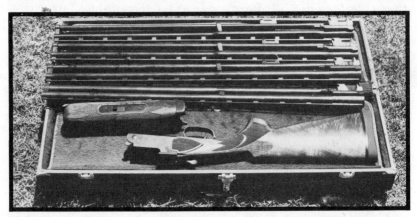

Fine guns should be carried in a leather or canvas case, at a minimum; aluminum cases provide superior protection.

duce several changes—in the chemical nature of the primer or charge, or in oxidation of the case or especially of lead bullets (indicated by a whitish color on the surface of the lead). Storage in a dark, dry, evenly-controlled temperature condition seems to retard aging.

Temperature changes, especially if extreme, can have mysterious and powerful effects upon ammunition. Heat is particularly damaging. When you travel by car, never carry ammunition in the trunk or glove compartment, or exposed to the heat inside the car on a hot day. Pack the ammunition in a styrofoam or other insulated chest and place it in a shaded area of the car floor, covered with blankets or other material to provide shade and additional insulation. Adding ice is not advised, as it usually results in condensation and moisture, and also in abnormally low temperatures. We believe that good ammunition, like good wine, should be stored at a constant temperature throughout its life.

Changes in air pressure also affect ammunition quality. This can be seen when ammunition is flown in unpressurized airplanes, or when it is carried to high altitudes where air pressure is very low. The results are sometimes bizarre and always unpredictable. Certain brands and/or lots seem less affected than others.

To paraphrase an old infantry maxim, take care of your guns and ammunition, and they will take care of you.

Weather
and Wind

I f you shoot outdoors, you'll inevitibly have to confront the effects of weather and wind. Unfortunately there's nothing that can be done to change conditions, and if you're hunting or entered in a scheduled competition, you may have no choice but to make the best of a bad situation. In such circumstances, a gritty attitude is invaluable. If you can say to yourself, "I'll succeed in spite of these obstacles," you're well ahead. The only alternatives are to make a half-hearted effort or to quit.

Water—such as rain, snow, mist, or moisture clinging to vegetation—can be troublesome in a number of ways. It washes dust and fine debris into the crevices of guns and sights and also causes rust. If it freezes, it can lock small mechanisms. The best prevention is to keep your equipment clean and the metal parts coated lightly with oil. After exposure to water, clean and re-oil. When not in use, telescopes can be protected with end-caps that keep the glass elements perfectly clean and dry.

Snow or chunks of ice in a gun barrel can cause it to rupture when fired. At the very least, small amounts of water in a gun barrel will affect accuracy. Take whatever precautions necessary to keep water out. Caution: do not plug the barrel; if you accidentally leave the plug in, the gun (and maybe you) may be permanently damaged.

Water also affects wood stocks, causing swelling and possibly warping. Protect wood with a sealer such as varnish, oil, or other waterproof finishes. No sealer is 100 percent effective, however. If your gun gets badly soaked, dismantle it, clean and oil the metal parts, and dry the wood by laying it in a well-ventilated place at room temperature. Never dry the wood in direct sunlight or with applied heat.

If you have to shoot in falling weather, you'll find a broad-brimmed hat or cap useful to keep water away from your eyes, glasses, and sights. A hat will also keep it from trickling down your neck—or at least some of it.

Temperature sometimes can have a bearing on accuracy. The metal of a gun expands in heat and contracts in cold. This may affect the gun's performance characteristics, particularly the accuracy of sight settings. If you calibrate your sights in moderate temperatures and are going to shoot in extremely hot or cold temperatures, test-fire in the new temperature to confirm the setting.

But of all environmental factors, wind is the most annoying to most shooters most of the time. Your best preparation is to become familiar with the effects of wind on your marksmanship. Sometimes you have no choice but to shoot in windy conditions, and the more experience you have in practice, the better you'll be able to perform when it counts.

Wind affects you by buffeting your body and by altering bullet trajectory. To protect yourself from buffeting, attempt, if possible, to use a sheltered firing point. Anything at all that breaks the wind will serve. Also, experiment with ways to "tighten" your position to reduce the effects of unavoidable buffeting. You can shorten the sling of a rifle, for example, and/or use increased muscle tension to make your position tighter and firmer to give increased stability in gusts.

The effects of wind on bullet trajectory are best understood by experience. The major effect is usually horizontal; but some gun-ammo combinations also respond with vertical changes in a cross-wind. This probably results from bullet spin; if so, it would be analogous to the effects of spin on a baseball speeding toward the plate. When this effect is seen, the bullet is usually moved toward 4 o'clock in a wind blowing from the left, and 10 o'clock in a wind blowing from the right (with right hand-twist barrels). Some smallbore shooters who experience the effect develop a formula for dealing with it; one common example is one click of vertical adjustment for every three clicks of horizontal adjustment. Since the vertical effect is not seen with all guns and ammo, however, this formula is not universally applicable. Experience with wind is the best way for you to determine if you need to use this or some other formula.

Cross-wind effects vary from range to range. A measured 10 mph wind will have one effect on one range or firing point, another somewhere else. This probably results from differences in ground-surface effects on low-moving air currents. Nevertheless, if you're so inclined, you can experiment with mathematical predictions of wind effects. While few shooters bother with this, it could prove useful in some situations. The best approach that we're familiar with was published in an article by Edward D. Lowry in the American Rifleman for June, 1962. At the time Lowry was manager of the Advance Research Section of the Winchester-Western Research Department. The article is reprinted here in its entirety. Note: the speed of match-grade .22 ammunition is about 1080 fps. This article was written for .22 standard velocity.

WIND DRIFT

By EDWARD D. LOWRY

ONE of the first things a shooter learns, to his chagrin, is that a sudden gust of wind can move his shot clean off the target. With practice he becomes reasonably proficient in compensating, even though he finds the whole question of wind drift a little puzzling. What principles, he asks, does the ballistician follow and how does he go about designing ammunition that minimizes wind drift? Does he choose a slow bullet that has comparatively little deceleration, or a fast bullet that gets to the target so quickly it doesn't have time to be deflected?

There are other interesting and more puzzling questions. Why, for example, is a .22 long rifle match bullet deflected 2 3/4" by a 10 f.p.s. cross wind over a 100-yd. range, while an identical bullet freely suspended in the same cross wind is deflected but a bare fraction of an inch during an equivalent .29-second flight time?

The answers to these questions lie within the deceptively simple wind drift formula. It states that wind drift is equal to cross wind velocity multiplied by lag time. The ballistician expresses this relationship in more precisely mathematical terms as:

D = $12v(T\text{-}R/V_0)$, where
D = drift in inches (by virtue of the factor 12),
v = cross wind velocity in feet per second (f.p.s.)
T = time of flight in seconds,
R = range in feet, and
V_0 = muzzle velocity, f.p.s.

The cross wind velocity depends on the instantaneous, unpredictable local meteorological conditions, and is therefore the uncontrollable term in the wind drift formula. The other term ($T\text{-}R/V_0$) is the lag time. It is to the ballistician the controllable term since its value depends on the aerodynamic efficiency of the bullet, its muzzle velocity, and the range. The wind drift characteristics of a bullet under given ballistic conditions can therefore be directly determined and effectually described by the value of this lag time term. Accordingly, we concentrate our attention on those factors which influence lag time.

For illustration, consider a train that leaves Station A at 60 miles an hour. Its next stop is Station B in 2 hours. Now for some reason or other the train gradually loses speed and arrives at Station B after 2 hours 15 minutes, or 15 minutes late. If we talked about trains this way, we'd say its lag time is 15 minutes.

Muzzle velocity of the .22 match bullet is 1120 f.p.s., so it should travel 300 ft. in $300/1120 = .268$ second. But, like the train, it loses speed and we know (by calculation and by measurement) that it actually takes .291 second to travel this range. Thus its lag time is .023 second, the amount of time the bullet is late. Using our formula, and assuming a 10 f.p.s. cross wind, we get

Wind drift = $(12)(10)(.291-.268) = 120(.023) = 2.76''$.

Let's now explore the basis of the wind drift formula. Again with the help of a railroad analogy, we can derive the formula with simple geometry.

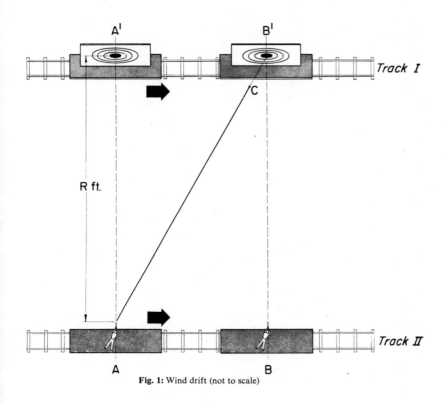

Fig. 1: Wind drift (not to scale)

Fig. 1 shows 2 railroad tracks which, we'll allow, are 300 ft. apart. A train is running on each track at a uniform speed of 10 f.p.s. Flatcars on the trains are directly abreast. On one, a shooter is firing with .22 long rifle ammunition at a target on the flatcar directly opposite him. The man fires while he and the target are on the line AA'. The bullet is given a forward velocity of 1120 f.p.s. by his gun and a lateral velocity of 10 f.p.s. by the train. Hence the bullet is launched on the path AB'. If there were no air resistance, the bullet and the target would arrive at B' simultaneously, .268 second later. However, the decelerating force of air resistance on the bullet prevents it maintaining its 1120 f.p.s. velocity and, accordingly, by the time the target reaches B' the bullet has only gone as far as the point C although it is still traveling straight toward B'. Since we know this bullet's lag time is .023 second, it will arrive at the point B' .023 second late. But the flatcar will maintain its constant 120 inch-per-second velocity. Hence, during the .023 second it takes the bullet to go from C to B', the target moves from B' to a point (120)(.023) or 2.76" farther down the track. The same situation applies if the cars remain stationary while a 10 f.p.s. wind blows from right to left.

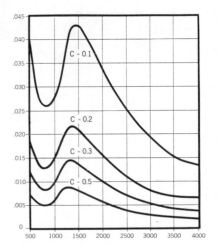

Fig 2: Lag time over 100 yds. vs. muzzle velocity for 4 ballistic coefficients

Analogy related

Referring again to Fig. 1, we relate the train analogy to our wind drift formula by considering that

v   is the flatcar velocity,
T   is the total time of flight (to go from Track II to Track I),
R   is the range (distance between tracks),
V_0 is the bullet's muzzle velocity.

Lag time

Before using the formula, however, we must overcome one difficulty. In the expression for lag time, the terms for range **R** and muzzle velocity **V** are usually known. The time of flight **T,** on the other hand, is generally not known and its calculation requires the availability of deceleration tables as well as accurate knowledge on the aerodynamic performance of the projectile. We can get around this difficulty by a simple

3-step procedure for an estimate of the lag time. Although the accuracy won't be sufficient to satisfy the ballistician, it can be used for getting an estimate within an error of not more than 15%. The procedure requires only that we know the physical characteristics of the bullet and its muzzle velocity. A 100-yd. range is assumed.

TABLE I

Estimation of form factor, i, of rifle bullets

$i = .60$ for very sharp profiles
$i = .70$ for moderately sharp profiles
$i = .85$ for moderately sharp profiles with bullet tip slightly flattened
$i = 1.00$ for moderately blunt profiles
$i = 1.20$ for very blunt profiles

NOTE: In using this table make the following corrections: If the bullet is boattailed, subtract .06 from the estimate of **i;** if it has a small exposed lead tip, like the .243 Winchester 100-gr. soft-point, add .07; if it has a large exposed lead tip, like the .257 Roberts 117-gr. soft-point, add .20.

The first step requires an estimate of a numerical index known as the form factor, **i.** This is a measure of the projectile's goodness of shape. For conventional rifle bullets the form factor varies from .54 for the .30-'06 Springfield 180-gr. boattail match bullet to 1.37 for the blunt lead-nosed 7 mm. Mauser 175-gr. bullet. The form factor for a given bullet can be very simply estimated by means of Table I. It should be noted that **i** is in no way related to bullet weight or diameter, as it is specifically a 'shape' index.

The second step requires calculation of the projectile's ballistic coefficient. The ballistic coefficient **C** is a measure of the

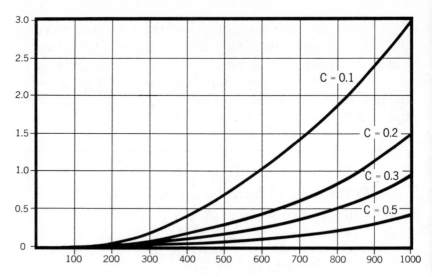

Fig. 3: Lag time vs. range at 3000 f.p.s. muzzle velocity

projectile's capacity to maintain its velocity in flight. It is given by the formula:

$$C = w/id^2,$$

where w = the projectile weight, in lbs.,
d = the projectile diameter, in inches,
i = the form factor

Since the weight w and the diameter d are accurately known, the formula is easily used once the form factor i has been estimated from Table I. As an example, consider the .243 Winchester 100-gr. soft-point bullet. Since one pound equals 7000 grs., the bullet's weight is .0143 lb. Its diameter is .2435″ and its form factor, as established by deceleration firings, is .67. The formula then says that this bullet's ballistic coefficient is:

$$C = \frac{w}{id^2} = \frac{.0143}{(.67)(.2435)^2} = .36.$$

The third step in the procedure gives us lag time. Since we know the muzzle velocity and have calculated the ballistic coefficient **C** we get lag time by simply interpolating between the curves of Fig. 2.

Behavior of bullets

These curves, incidentally, show a very interesting relationship. It will be noted that for very slow bullets, the lag time is quite high. As the muzzle velocity approaches 800 or 850 f.p.s., the lag time hits a low. As the velocity is further increased, the lag time again goes up and with still further increases in muzzle velocity, the lag time decreases continuously. The somewhat bizarre behavior of these curves is a consequence of the complex behavior of a projectile as it approaches and then exceeds sonic speed.

Now that we can estimate the lag time with reasonable accuracy, we need but know the cross wind velocity to compute wind drift. For obtaining comparative bullet performance we simply assume some constant wind velocity, generally 10 f.p.s., and compute the comparative drifts. The following table gives a useful rough index of relative strength of winds (to convert, note that 30 miles per hour is equal to 44 f.p.s.):

5 f.p.s.— Very light breeze
10 f.p.s.— Light breeze, leaves rustle, leaves and small twigs begin to move
20 f.p.s.— Moderate breeze, extends light flags and begins to move branches, raises dust and loose paper
30 f.p.s.— Fresh breeze, forms small-crested waves, small trees in leaf begin to sway
40 f.p.s.— Strong breeze, whistles in telephone wires, large branches in motion
50 f.p.s.— Moderate gale, sways whole trees, hard to walk against wind

Fig. 3 shows how lag time varies as the range increases. From aerodynamic considerations, lag time should be roughly proportional to the square of the range. Thus the lag time at 200 yds. should be 4 times that at 100 yds., that at 300 yds. should be 9 times that at 100 yds., etc. As can be seen from Fig. 3, this relationship holds true within a rather small error.

Questions on lag time

Now that we have a somewhat simple understanding of lag time and can estimate it with fairly reasonable accuracy, let's investigate a few fundamental questions.

We have already mentioned the discrepancy in the comparative drift of a freely suspended bullet and one in flight. This question can be partially answered by our now familiar railroad analogy. Suppose that in our analogy we use the same rimfire match bullet but reduce both its muzzle velocity and the range to one-tenth the values originally taken. In other words, the muzzle velocity is only 112 f.p.s. while the distance between tracks is only 30 ft. The 'scheduled' time will of course be the same since $30/112 = 300/1120 = .268$ second. However, since the force of air resistance is roughly proportional to the square of the velocity, the decelerating force on the bullet in this instance is only about a hundredth as much as when the projectile starts off at 1120 f.p.s. Accordingly, the bullet is decelerated very little. Applying this to Fig. 1, the point C is much closer to B' since the bullet has been decelerated very slightly. It actually travels the 30 ft. distance in just less than .269 second, which means that its lag time is less than .001 second. Hence, by our formula:

Drift = (12)(10)(.001 −) = less than .12″

Carrying the illustration farther, consider a bullet that is picked up off a table and then dropped. The bullet will travel 14″ during .268 second. It is easy to visualize that a lateral deflection of this dropped bullet in a 10 f.p.s. wind could not exceed a small fraction of an inch.

Another question might be the following: "What sort of bullet should I choose to minimize wind drift—a large-caliber heavy bullet to minimize air resistance, a small-caliber light bullet with a very high muzzle velocity, or a small-caliber heavy bullet of high sectional density?"

What happens

The answer to this question can be obtained by straightforward calculation, but is easier visualized by reference to Fig. 4. We know, for example, that a small-diameter bullet, due to the limitations on its length and therefore its weight, cannot be given the same kinetic energy as a bullet of larger diameter. Accordingly, we have picked, for comparison, 2 well-known calibers. In one case we choose a bullet with the same propellant charge as the .243 Winchester 80-gr. which has a muzzle energy of 2180 ft.-lbs. With the 80-gr. bullet we get a muzzle velocity of 3500 f.p.s. In the second case we take the .308 Winchester 150-gr. with a fixed assumed muzzle energy of 2730 ft.-lbs. This larger 150-gr. bullet has a muzzle velocity of 2860 f.p.s. It is quickly apparent from the figure that the bullet of smaller diameter, and even of lower muzzle energy, gives a smaller lag time. However, we also know that for the same muzzle energy a slight reduction in lag time is obtained by increasing the bullet weight. We can generalize these results into 2 conclusions that tell us we can minimize lag time by: (1) going to the lowest possible projectile diameter that we can for a given amount of propellant (that is, a fixed muzzle energy); and (2) using the longest bullet which is practical for the caliber.

For a third question someone might ask, "What happens when you shoot straight up?" Most people who have tried this claim that they never see the bullet come down, at least nowhere in the immediate vicinity. What sort of effect could wind drift have on deflecting this bullet? Suppose we took for our example the .30-'06 Springfield 150-gr. Silvertip. It has a muzzle velocity of 2970 f.p.s. and a ballistic coefficient of .31. Fired straight up, it will take 18.1 seconds for the bullet to rise to its maximum height of 8317 ft. We can immediately compute lag time as:

$(\mathbf{T\text{-}R}/\mathbf{V_0}) = (18.1 - 8317/2970) = (18.1 - 2.8) =$ 15.3 seconds

This means that in a 10 f.p.s. cross wind, the bullet would be deflected $10 \times 15.3 = 153$ ft. at the summit. (Actually, the wind drift formula is being overstrained in this application, but it does help illustrate the effect.) By the time the projectile has reached the summit it has almost completely picked up the lateral wind velocity. Since this bullet will take about 45 seconds to make its descent, it will travel an additional lateral distance which might be as much as $10 \times 45 = 450$ ft. Its total lateral deflection by the time it hits the ground is then a few hundred feet, due to wind drift alone. There are other reasons why the bullet might not come right back to its point of origin, but this example shows how even a light breeze can deflect a bullet by a distance great enough so the shooter would never detect its return to the ground.

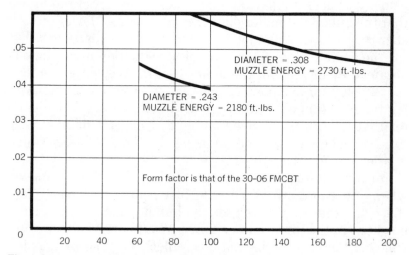

Fig. 4: Lag time over 300 meters vs. bullet weight for bullets of the same form factor and 2 muzzle energies at 2 diameters

7
Gunmanship

We would like now to consider values that go beyond standards of consistency and accuracy.

Gunmanship, loosely defined, is the ability, character, and methods of one who handles guns. We are deeply concerned that poor gunmanship poses a serious threat to the Constitutional rights of U. S. citizens to own and use arms. Poor gunmanship is responsible for the growing sentiment in favor of gun-control legislation or a Constitutional amendment to prohibit gun ownership.

Part of the problem is that good gunmanship attracts no notice. The public at large has virtually no way of knowing how many guns are used in the U. S. every day for perfectly good utilitarian and recreational purposes. What they do know about, however, are the instances in which guns are used in the commission of crimes; and they also know about the instances of poor gunmanship they themselves see, instances that may or may not be strictly illegal, but are nevertheless undesirable. These are two entirely separate issues, and it is important to distinguish between them and to address them separately.

In the public's mind, the most clear-cut instance of poor gunmanship is the use of firearms for criminal purposes. A kind of knee-jerk reaction to this is to propose to outlaw guns, on the theory that if all guns were confiscated, then firearm-related crimes would cease. Fortunately, most well-informed individuals can see the fallacy of this argument. To begin with, criminals would not surrender guns in a confiscation program. Further, confiscation would not work for the same reasons that Prohibition did not work. The world-wide supply of armaments is vast, and their availability and the ease with which they could be smuggled across our borders would create a lucrative black market. In addition, any knowledgeable person is aware that guns of very high quality can be produced even by a hobbyist with a modestly equipped home workshop. In this day and age, a criminal who wants a gun can get one whether guns are outlawed or not. This is simply a fact we must all live with.

So in dealing with blatant criminal use of firearms, restrictive gun-control legislation is pointless. However, it is not pointless in dealing with other forms of poor gunmanship among the more law-abiding segment of our population, and people realize this. And herein lies our major concern. We will deal with just two types of poor gunmanship—unnecessary display and reckless use.

The unnecessary display of guns often results from the gun-owner's conviction that gun-ownership is a Constitutional right and, damn it, he will carry a gun wherever he pleases and those who don't like it will just have to get used to it. Where the law permits, he displays a gun on a rack in his vehicle or carries it on his person.

While this attitude may be strictly legal, it nevertheless fails to take into account the emotional responses many people have to guns, and it only inflames anti-gun sentiments.

Whether rationally or not, many people are terrified of guns. A strictly rational person looks at a gun in much the same way as a Wimbledon champion looks at a tennis racquet —it is an instrument for sport, a tool to accomplish a given purpose. But many people have been conditioned to equate guns with brutality, war, crime, victimization, violence, and bloodshed. These conditioned feelings are often quite deep and strong. When such people see a gun displayed in public, they react with disgust and even terror. They ask themselves a perfectly logical question: "Why is that person displaying a gun? Does he intend to use it against me or some other victim?"

Quite frankly, the unnecessary display of a gun *is* intimidating, even to those without irrational fears. The needless display of guns makes those who fear guns even more vociferous in their call for gun-controls; and it makes those more rational people, who were formerly neutral, more inclined to agree that gun-control might be worthwhile.

Our advice: never display a gun unnecessarily, even where it is perfectly legal.

The second glaring instance of poor gunmanship is the reckless use of firearms. Let's cite some typical examples.

A farmer with good hunting land does not post his property and has no objection to legal hunting. A careless hunter mistakenly shoots one of his cattle.

Each hunting season, the residents of a rural area see most of the road signs disfigured or destroyed by bullet holes. They know that their tax dollars are used to replace the signs, which cost many hundreds of dollars.

A farm wife drives up to her house with two small children. As they get out of the car, someone in a woods a half-mile away begins firing a high-powered rifle over the house. She rushes the children inside, all three terrified.

A group of hunters from the city enter the woods and spend the entire day without seeing game. When they gather at their vehicle, they have a few drinks and, driving out, decide to shoot the windows out of an "abandoned" building.

Every time incidents like these occur—and they are common—a few more people change their minds in favor of gun-control. Unfortunately, the number of people making this change is alarmingly high. And who is to blame?

Almost all of the reckless use of guns is attributable to two related causes. One is that some people mistakenly believe that if you arm yourself and go into the woods and fields, you are a "hunter." These people have no idea of what hunting is all about. To them, you go hunting to "shoot," and to "kill something." We're in favor of weeding these people out of the hunting population by a licensing system similar to those that have been used successfully in Europe for decades. An applicant seeking a license must pass qualifying tests similar to those currently used in issuing driving licenses. Most European countries recognize that hunting is not a right, but a privilege that must be earned, and we support that view.

Associated with ignorance of hunting is the desire of some to "use" their guns. This is perfectly understandable. A person who has invested several hundred dollars in a fine gun naturally wants to shoot it. After spending one or two days of precious vacation time in the woods and seeing no game, the individual is likely to take out his frustrations by shooting at something else—beer cans, road signs, or what-have-you. The frustration that seeks release in this way often stems from an unrealistic expectation about hunting—the mistaken belief that game is abundant and easily found even by someone who just stumbles into the woods. As every good hunter knows, this is simply not the case.

We have a recommendation. Admittedly, it is probably biased because of our own interests and experience. But it is this: if you're interested in guns, consider taking up competitive marksmanship.

Obviously, we have no objection to guns. But we do feel that the share of habitat available to wild game is constantly shrinking at the same time that more and more people want to own and use guns. If you enjoy shooting, hunting is a poor way to pursue the interest, for if you're a good marksman, the number of times you'll actually fire a gun is severely limited by hunting seasons and bag limits. With some game species, you'll be limited to one shot per year.

On the other hand, you can enjoy competitive marksmanship year-round and fire a gun as often as you want. Firing at competitive targets will enable you to become truly an expert with a gun; and it is a social activity in which you can involve your friends and family; it is a lifetime sport which you can enjoy from ages 9 to 90; and, properly conducted, it does nothing to fuel anti-gun sentiment among the non-shooting public. In fact, by introducing people to competitive marksmanship, you can easily persuade them to a pro-gun position.

By competitive marksmanship we do not necessarily mean organized and sanctioned matches. All that is necessary is that you have a safe firing range where you can use guns without annoyance to others. You can shoot at something as

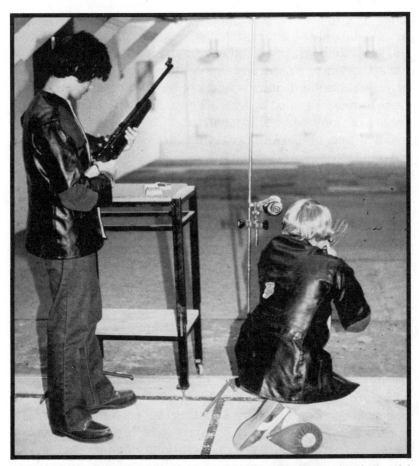

Target shooting appeals to men and women from youth to old age. It is a social activity that brings friends and families together in a common interest. Indoor range facilities allow evening schedules, as well as affording protection from weather.

commonplace as drink cans, but regulation paper targets provide a much more accurate indication of shooting skill, are readily available, and are inexpensive. Once you've built a simple target frame, your range is complete. You can shoot to your heart's content and teach your family and children to shoot safely and well.

If you're on a limited budget or have limited space, consider air-guns (rifles and pistols). A complete range can be installed inside an average house, pellets cost very little, and the lead can be trapped and recycled. Modern target air-guns have short-range accuracy capabilities equal to the best modern conventional firearms and are built to resemble conventional guns in realistic detail. They lack only the recoil and report of conventional firearms.

Of course, one of the great pleasures of target shooting is competition with other shooters. Gun clubs exist in most cities and towns, and existing clubs are usually quite helpful in introducing newcomers to the sport. For a list of gun-clubs in your area, consult a local gun dealer or write to the Competitions Division, National Rifle Association, 1600 Rhode Island Ave. N. W., Washington, D. C. 20036.

If no gun club exists in your area and you would like to organize one, the NRA will provide guidelines, instructional material, and even range plans. Write to the above address for information.

If you have never participated in competitive shooting, you probably will be surprised to learn how well-organized and widespread it is. Competitive shooting receives little publicity in the major news media because media executives are reluctant to publicize the "controversial" firearms sports, for one reason. For another, shooting sports have very little spectator appeal. They are sports which people attend in order to participate, not to watch. Many competitive shooters, conscious of the negative reactions of some people to shooting sports, intentionally keep a "low profile" and avoid public attention.

As you probably know, almost every major amateur sport is controlled by a national governing body which in turn belongs to an international federation. In the U. S., the national governing body is the National Rifle Association, which in turn belongs to a world-wide federation, the International Shooting Union (ISU). The NRA provides its own set of rules for marksmanship events, sanctions matches, verifies and maintains records, and performs a host of other functions necessary to maintaining and promoting national amateur shooting sports programs.

NRA sanctions events at local, state, regional, and national levels, with the National Match Championships taking place each summer, attended by thousands of marksmen of all ages and walks of life from across the U. S.

Beyond these events, the NRA fields teams for ISU sanctioned international matches, the major ones being the Pan-American Games, The World Games, The Championship of the Americas, and the Olympic Games. There are also numerous invitational matches that take place each year in this country and abroad, all conducted according to ISU rules.

Within the U. S., organized shooting programs exist for men and women, adults and juniors. Qualified instructors and prepared instructional materials introduce young people (as well as adults) to the sport safely and effectively.

What are the different kinds of competitive events? Well, just about every kind. Our own interests lie in international (ISU) style competition, which is standard almost everywhere in the world. International style events include:

Shotgun:	skeet Olympic trap automatic trap
Pistol:	rapid fire pistol center fire pistol standard pistol ladies pistol free pistol air pistol
Rifle:	smallbore free rifle smallbore standard rifle air rifle big-bore free rifle

big-bore standard rifle
running game

Current rule books for NRA and ISU style events may be ordered from the Competitions Division, National Rifle Association, 1600 Rhode Island Ave. N. W., Washington, D. C. 20036.

You might also be interested in a series of booklets on the above events written and published by the United States Army Marksmanship Unit, Fort Benning, Georgia 31905. The booklets are "how-to" literature and are suitable for use as instructional materials or for self-teaching. You may request a free booklet by writing to the Commanding Officer. Please limit the request to booklets on shooting events you are genuinely interested in, remembering that they are financed with tax dollars and that the paper they are printed on is made from trees.

The AMU is the center for advanced marksmanship in the U. S. We will have more to say about it on page 192.

The rest of this book will be directed primarily to target shooting, though it will have relevance to other forms of marksmanship such as those used in hunting, law-enforcement, and the military. But if you're wondering how you can become a local, state, national, or world champion in target shooting, or how you can coach a person toward such a goal, the rest of this book will map the way.

We'll discuss the subject at perhaps its highest level—the production of an Olympic champion. The program we outline will thus appear rather rigorous, perhaps more rigorous than you care to follow. Just remember that you don't have to be an Olympic champion to be a successful shooter—you can operate at any level you choose, and if you meet the goals you set for yourself, you're successful. So feel free to modify any of the issues we discuss in order to adapt them to your own goals. However, the same principles we outline will apply no matter what level of development you reach.

8
Equipment for
Target Shooting

hether you wish to shoot alone on your private range or enter sanctioned competitive events, your enjoyment and proficiency in target shooting will be increased if you have certain helpful or even necessary items of equipment beyond a gun, ammunition, and target. The best way to become familiar with these items is to watch experienced shooters at work, either in practice or in actual matches. Competitive events are more informative to watch because you get to observe a number of shooters' equipment.

The best models to follow in equipment are the first-rate shooters, those who win matches and championships and gold medals. They are the experienced individuals who know how to achieve maximum performance using only essential equipment.

Observe the better shooters and find out what they use. If you're friendly and approach them in a candid and honest fashion, most will take the time to talk with you about equipment. Do this at a time, however, when the individual is not engaged in a serious training session, in match preparation, or in a match itself. As we'll see later, most advanced shooters do not want to be disturbed during the hours preceeding a match, for this interrupts their mental preparation. The best time to approach a shooter is a day or two before, or, even better, shortly after he has completed a match. But you don't really need to talk to the person if you're only interested in what he's using. You can usually find out what you want to know just by looking.

A word of caution. There is a mild trendiness in shooting equipment just as there are fashions and fads in almost everything else. Accessories that were "in" last year will be "out" next year. Try not to be seduced by these trends, which are usually most visibly displayed by persons with a great deal of stylishness and panache in equipment, but mediocre performances on the firing line. If you're interested in becoming a good marksman and not just a fashion plate, ignore such people when it comes to advice about equipment. Listen instead to winning marksmen.

Even more insidious than fashionability is the allure of gadgeteering. Gadgeteering is the belief that scores can be miraculously improved through the use of a new item or gadget. You can get so wrapped up in shopping for, buying, and experimenting with new items that you almost completely forget about working on performance skills. We believe that the road to shooters' hell is paved with millions of gadgets of all types and descriptions. Fortunately, championship shooting is not to be achieved with gadgets, for then gold medals could simply be awarded to those who had the most money to purchase the most gadgets. Championship performance is achieved through training and work spent in developing human performance skills.

If you wish to avoid trendiness and gadgeteering, we recommend that you buy and use only the minimum, essential items. This is not only less expensive; it also simplifies your shooting procedures and cuts down on the number of items you have to keep track of and think about. Your mind is freed to do its proper task—to concentrate on your performance. Buy good quality items that will function well over a number of years, then use them with good judgment and a certain decorum. You will not regret this.

Before purchasing any item for use in sanctioned competitions, you should refer to a current rulebook for the type of matches you've chosen to enter. Make sure the rulebook is current. Rules do change from year to year, and from NRA to ISU style matches.

The first thing you'll need, or course, is a gun. For sanctioned matches, this is almost always a gun designed or prepared exclusively for target shooting. If it's a handgun or rifle, you'll want it equipped with good quality adjustable target sights. If you're a beginner, you'll do best to stay with production-line stocks or grips. Only after you've had a year

Everyone engaging in conventional firearm marksmanship should wear hearing protectors. Either muff-type or inserts are available.

or two of experience, and given the matter considerable study, should you progress to altering the stock or grips for improved fit or control. Many good shooters never alter the contours of stocks and grips because the production-line models fit them almost perfectly. If you need an alteration, however, and what you contemplate is legal, there is no reason not to have it done if it will improve your performance. Do give it study, however, for most alterations are irreversible.

Now, let's list the minimum items you'll need besides a gun, ammunition, targets, and range facilities.

Shotgun:	rulebook
	shotgun and case
	gun cleaning equipment
	shooting glasses
	hearing protectors
	shooting vest or jacket
	notebook and pen
Handgun:	rulebook
	handgun(s) and case(s)
	gun cleaning equipment
	tool kit (screwdrivers for

sight & trigger adjustments,
etc.)
shooting glasses
hearing protectors
spotting scope and tripod
stopwatch
ammo block
notebook and pen

Rifle:

rulebook
rifle(s) and case(s)
gun cleaning equipment
tool kit (screwdrivers for
sight & trigger adjustment,
etc.)
shooting glasses
hearing protectors
spotting scope tripod and
extensions
stopwatch
ammo block
equipment box
shooting jacket(s)
notebook and pen
shooting scope*
shooting glove*
sling (good quality leather)*
handstop*
palm rest*
butt plate*
butt hook*
prone plate*
balance weight*
kneeling roll*
shooting mat*

---

*Depending on the events you enter.

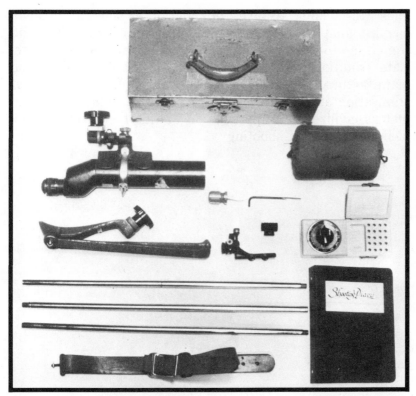

Part of a rifle shooter's gear. Clockwise, from top: equipment box, kneeling roll, ammo box and stopwatch, diary, leather sling, tripod extensions for spotting scope, scope stand, spotting scope. In center, simple tools and detachable sights.

There are, of course, many other items that you can buy, some of them moderately useful, many of them most useful in putting money in the manufacturers' pockets. If you find an additional item that is genuinely useful and legal, however, don't hesitate to buy and use it. In shooting, as in any sport, the equipment is not an end in itself, but the means to an end.

We would be remiss to end this discussion without mentioning that shooting gear often has a strong aesthetic appeal. Rich wood tones, burnished metal, and pure, functional lines can combine to give guns and other shooting gear an elegant simplicity that is frequently quite beautiful and something to be enjoyed in its own right by those who appreciate tradition, good design, fine craftmanship, and good manufacture. Fine shooting equipment is just as worthy of admiration as fine furniture or beautiful architecture, and just as civilized. An appreciation of this fact is one of the basic pleasures of shooting.

9 Position Building

A solid, stable position is essential to successful target shooting. If the position is to be used throughout a standard string of fire, it must also be durable, which means that it must be reasonably comfortable and require a minimum expenditure of energy. If your position is uncomfortable or involves excessive muscular effort, the result will almost always be degeneration of performance as you progress through the string of fire. And of course, last but not least, any position must be legal as defined by NRA or ISU rules.

The best way of teaching or learning shooting positions is to begin with "average" positions. These are the positions most often described in books and manuals, and for this reason are known among shooters as "book" positions. They are not entirely abstractions; the percentage of shooters with average body builds almost precisely reproduce the positions when firing. Others depart from book positions in varying degrees, for reasons which will be made clear in a moment.

During his or her first lessons, a beginner should always attempt to assume a book position. This should be done without regard to the natural aim-point of the gun. In fact, during this initial experimental stage, it is even desirable to work without a target or sights and to concentrate solely on building a facsimile book position. At this stage, whether the gun points above or below the target is irrelevant.

The reasons for this are two-fold. First, by experiencing a book position, the beginner is assured of acquiring familiarity with a position that meets all the requirements of legality, reasonable comfort, and minimum energy expenditure. Being familiar with the feel of these positions is important in both beginning and later stages of development. Second, he or she will be establishing a known, easily reconstructed starting point from which to begin the possibly complex later task of position building and refining.

Once a book position has been established and you have become familiar with the feel of it—usually in the second or third session—you can address the problem of natural aim point. A natural aim point, as we indicated earlier in the book, is the point at which the gun aims when the position is making maximum use of bone support, or to state it another way, when minimum muscular effort is being expended. For some people, a book position will yield a natural aim point that centers exactly on the target. If you fall into this category, be quick to give thanks, for your task in building a position is immeasurably simplified.

The shooter whose book position does not yield a natural aim point on the target has two means of addressing the problem. The first and most desirable is by adjusting the dimensions of the gun, if this is possible or legal. To the maximum extent possible, a gun should fit the shooter's body conformations, and not the other way around. In all but unusual cases, this can be accomplished by choosing a gun stock that fits the individual user; in most cases, production-line stock models are available in the required dimensions.

If production stocks are not available, then you are faced with the alternative of cutting away or building up the stock, a task which, except in very simple form, should not be undertaken lightly, for two very good reasons. First, this type of alteration is usually irretrievable and will probably reduce the resale value of the stock to zero. But perhaps more importantly, an alteration that appears to be desirable initially may, in practice, be the wrong one, so that not only the resale value but also the intrinsic value of the stock is lost forever. Permanent alterations are best reserved until the shooter is in an advanced intermediate stage of development and can make very precise judgments about the effects of even minor changes in stock configurations.

In a percentage of cases, however, neither factory stock dimensions nor even intelligently customized stocks will yield a natural aim point at the target. Or you may find that the classic book position is not quite right for you, not as stable and steady as you would like because it is unsuited to your body contours. In either situation, you are faced with the very difficult task of systematically modifying the book position to correct the problem. The task is difficult because, unless done with keen insight, it will quite possibly result in a loss of some component of steadiness, comfort, minimum energy expenditure, or legality.

On the other hand, approached with a great deal of care and thought, and executed systematically, position building is one of the keys to successful shooting. Refinements in your position can lead to improved stability, greater precision in performance, and therefore higher scores. Most shooters do at least some position building, if only to introduce refinements.

We must stress that position building is always a unique and completely personalized project. No one can tell you what changes you should make, nor should you make a change in order to copy the position of another successful shooter. What works for someone else will probably not work for you, and vice versa. When you embark on building your own best position, you are beginning a journey that has never been made before, a unique journey into your own body and mind in relation to your own particular gun. You must discover your weaknesses, logically arrive at probable solutions, and design the changes that implement the solutions. What works for you is right for you. If a particular change works for you, don't hesitate to adopt it even though it may be unorthodox. In position building, systematic analysis is not only the major thing, it is the only thing. And if your analysis is right, the fact that it's different means only that you're capable of original thought.

Naturally, you'll check your rulebook first to see if the change is legal. This seems obvious, but every year individuals are disqualified in important matches because some piece of equipment or some feature of their positions is illegal. This is an embarrassing experience, even humiliating; still worse, it's demoralizing too because it means that months of training time have gone needlessly down the drain. *Check your rulebook.*

If you're smart—and we know you are, because you're reading this book—you'll realize at once that position building should be a completely scientific affair, characterized by complete objectivity, rigid controls, and meticulous evaluation. All of which means that to a certain type of analytical mind, it can be a fascinating challenge and great fun. You can have fun and be a mediocre shooter even if you aren't interested in the scientific method. But you can have fun and be a really good shooter only if you have the cast of mind that delights in problem solving and enjoys scientific analysis. World-class shooters are invariably men and women with these intellectual traits.

One of the primary concerns of the experimental scientist is to eliminate random influences from his experiments. He wishes to have complete control of every variable in his experimental system, and thus test his hypothesis by changing one variable in the system, and only one. In this way, he can isolate and evaluate the effects of that one, single variable with reasonable certainty.

So it is with the shooter. He wants to know with reasonable certainty the effect of any change he makes in his positions. To do this, he must follow certain simple rules:

1. Establish your own basic position. This may be a book position or some modification of it. Then assume the same position every time you shoot until you modify it according to the rules which follow.

   Your memory of the position is not a sufficient guide. Write a detailed description of it in your shooting diary, which will be one of your most useful analytical tools. If you have a coach, he should observe your position and become familiar with it in detail. Have photographs taken of it from various angles. If it's a standing position, mark the position of your feet on the floor with tape, or, even better, stand on a sheet of paper and outline your footprints with a pencil. Do the same for points of contact in the kneeling and prone positions, and use the marks for reference each time you begin a new session. Mark the points of contact between your body and the gun by applying masking tape and making pencil marks on the tape. Do the same for the positions of the sling adjustments, butt hook, palm rest, fore-end stop, etc., as references for future sessions. Design whatever system of records you like, but keep one goal in mind: you want to assume the exact same position every time you shoot, until you make a modification.

After you've had several weeks of experience, you'll be able to leave aside such obvious aids as guidemarks on the floor, but you will probably continue to mark tape on your gun and maintain a careful diary.

2. Make no change until you have identified a problem and arrived at its probable solution.

Another side of this is that you make no random changes. Make changes only for specific reasons, with specific results in mind. Perhaps you feel unstable and believe that your stability would improve if you placed your feet closer together (or further apart). Or perhaps you believe that changing the position of the grip of your trigger hand would result in a smoother release. Whatever the situation, do not make a change until you know why a change is desirable and what the change should be.

3. Record the change.

Make new marks on the floor or paper to show the changed position of your feet, if you still are in the beginning stage and using this device. Make marks on the tape to show the changed position of your trigger hand. Record the change in your diary, along with any changes that result in your performance.

4. Make only one change at a time.

If you change the position of your feet and the position of your trigger hand at the same time, how can you tell the effect of either on your performance? Your performance may get better or it may get worse, but why? Quite frankly, you don't know the exact single reason, and you cannot know. Change only one thing at a time, however, and you can make a judgment with reasonable certainty. If the change results in improvement, fine—adopt it. If it results in no change or a deterioration in performance, go back to your original position (thankfully recorded) and start over.

5. Evaluate the results of the change carefully.

Sometimes a change is the right one, but the effects will not show up until the second or third shooting session. On the other hand, the change may be a wrong one and the effects will not show up until later. So give any change at least three training sessions before making a judgment about it. Write a separate evaluation of it in your diary for each session.

Even trickier is the unpredictable effect of a

change in competition as opposed to training. Sometimes changes that work fine in training sessions prove to be unworkable in competition. The final test of a position change is to use it in actual competition and see if it leads to better scores.

6. If a change is rejected, return to your previous position before making another change.

   If you make a change, reject it, move directly to another change and reject it, pretty soon you'll have departed completely from your basic position and so many uncontrolled variables will have crept into your system that you will have lost the element of certainty. If you reject a change and go back to the position you used before the change was made, however, you retain the element of certainty in evaluating future changes.

In summary,

1. Establish your own basic position.

2. Make no change until you have identified a problem and arrived at its probable solution.

3. Record the change.

4. Make only one change at a time.

5. Evaluate the results of the change carefully.

6. If a change is rejected, return to your previous position before making another change.

You should follow these or similar procedures throughout your shooting career, which may last an adult lifetime. In fact, the more advanced you become, the more meticulous you'll become about applying the scientific method with great rigor.

You'll notice two things as you progress in your position building. One is that as a beginner, the changes and adjustments you make in your position are of relatively large proportions. You may change the position of your feet by three or four inches, for example, or you may change the way you face toward the target by ten to twenty degrees. But as you refine the position over the months and years. the changes become smaller and smaller, more and more finely tuned. A change in the position of your feet may be a quarter of an inch; you may change the way you face toward or away from the target by two or three degrees. As a beginner, your changes will be visible to an observer; as an advanced shooter, what you consider an important, significant change may be totally invisible to even the keenest observer.

The other thing you'll notice as you progress is a growing awareness of your body and its functions as you shoot. Initially, as a new beginner, you will be aware only of the gross features of your position, the weight of the gun, and the larger muscle groups controlling the balance of your body and the gun. But slowly, gradually, imperceptibly, you will become more and more aware of your body until the most delicate shifts in balance can be felt in the balls of your feet, you legs, spine, and neck. You will be aware that a minute shift in position can throw control of the balanced weight of the gun onto an entirely different set of minor muscles; and you will be able to sense tension in an individual muscle, and even in a segment of muscle, in isolation from its surrounding group. This growing awareness of your body is what enables you to make intelligent position changes; it is in fact central to the act of shooting and we will return to this topic repeatedly in later sections of the book.

Now we'll summarize the book positions for shotgun, handgun, and rifle competitions. You can find more detailed discussions of book positions in the following free publications available from the USAMU, Fort Benning, Georgia 31905: *The International Skeet and Trap Guide; Pistol Marksmanship Guide; Basic Smallbore Rifle Guide; International Rifle Marksmanship Guide; International Running Target Guide.*

All descriptions are for right-handed shooters.

Shotgun

Skeet

1. The feet should be a comfortable distance apart, the left foot slightly forward of the right. The

The skeet shooter's ready position. Note the alert but relaxed attitude.

toes may point slightly outward. The gunner is usually facing about 45 degrees to the right of the line on which he expects to shoot.

2. The right leg should be straight, but the knee should not be locked. The left knee should be slightly bent, and the left foot should bear much of the body's weight during the swing. Some shooters prefer to keep most body weight on the right foot until bringing the gun to the shoulder; others like to keep weight on the left foot even while standing at the ready position.

3. The gun is held in the ready position in both hands, with the butt held near the right hip and the muzzle elevated at a comfortable, natural angle.

A skeet shooter in action.

4. As the gun is brought to the shoulder, the torso is bent slightly forward from the hips; this bend is maintained during the swing and follow-through.

The stance, swing, and follow-through should be characterized by a feeling of balance and an easy, fluid motion free of excessive muscular tension.

Trap

1. The feet should be a comfortable distance apart, the left foot slightly forward of the right. The toes may point slightly outward. The gunner usually faces about 45 degrees to the right of the line on which he expects to shoot.

The trap shooter's ready position. Note the weight on the forward foot and the slight forward bend from the waist.

2. The right leg should be straight, but the knee not locked. The left knee should be slightly bent, and the left foot should bear much of the body's weight.

3. The gun should be held at the shoulder, aiming comfortably and naturally toward a point below the expected appearance of the target. The torso should be bent forward slightly from the hips.

    The stance, swing, and follow-through should be characterized by a feeling of balance and easy, fluid motion free of excessive muscular tension.

Handgun

1. The feet should be a comfortable distance apart, with the toes pointing slightly outward. An average distance between the feet is about shoulder-width, but the distance may be slightly more or less. Weight should be about equally distributed on both feet. Most shooters face about 70 to 90 degrees to the left of the target.

2. The legs should be straight, but the knees should not be rigidly locked.

3. The right arm should point the gun at the target in as natural a way as possible, neither too relaxed nor too rigid.

4. The head should be perfectly vertical, with no tilt forward, backward, or to the side.

5. The left arm should be relaxed. The left hand may rest in a pocket, on a belt, against the hip, or hang loosely at the side.

Like all marksmen, pistol shooters learn to relax between relays without losing concentration.

6. The torso should be bent from the hips to the left and slightly back in order to move the center of gravity of the body-gun complex directly over a point between the feet. The hips may be kept directly over the feet, or moved slightly in the direction of the target.

7. The right hand should grasp the pistol in such a way as to meet the following requirements:

a. it is comfortable

b. it is steady

c. it allows for perfect sight alignment

d. it allows for a trigger pull that does not disturb sight alignment or sight picture

e. it absorbs recoil without twisting, and transmits recoil directly back to the arm and shoulder

Some experimentation may be necessary to discover the proper position of the hand. Customized or different grips on the pistol may facilitate finding a proper hand position when difficulties arise in adjusting to a new gun.

Rifle

Standing position

1. The feet should be a comfortable distance apart, toes pointing slightly outward. An average distance apart is about shoulder width, but the distance may be slightly more or less. Most shooters face between 45 and 90 degrees to the right of the target. Weight should be distributed about evenly on both feet.

2. The left arm utilizes bone support to carry much of the weight of the rifle. The upper left arm should rest against the rib cage; the forearm should angle up to enable the left hand to meet the palm rest, if a free-rifle is used, or to enable the left hand to meet the stock if a standard rifle is used. With a standard rifle, the gun may rest

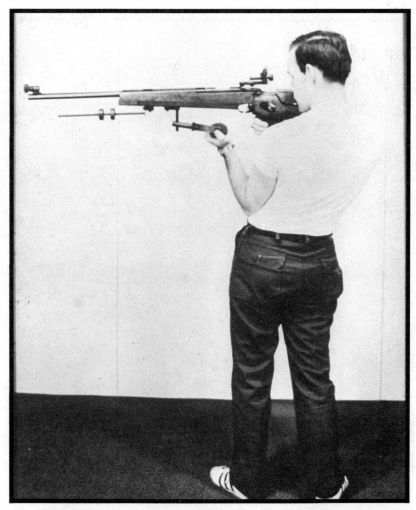

The back bend and twist bring the center of gravity directly over the feet. The shooter's jacket has been removed to illustrate the position.

on the fingertips, between extended fingers, or on top of a balled fist.

3. The torso is twisted to the left and bent back over the right hip to bring the center of gravity

Good Shooting
Lones W. Wigger Jr.

A free-rifle shooter shows solid position.

of the body-rifle complex directly over a point between the feet. This brings the complex into a state of balance or equilibrium. The head should be held vertically, with no tilt forward, backward, or to the side.

4. The right hand grasps the stock behind the trigger guard and pulls the gun back against the right shoulder. With a free-rifle, some of this work is performed by the butt hook, and the right hand may grip the stock very lightly. The right elbow may be raised almost to shoulder height, or may drop naturally an an angle from the shoulder, or occupy an intermediate position, whatever feels comfortable. The position of the right hand should allow for a trigger pull that does not disturb the aim of the gun.

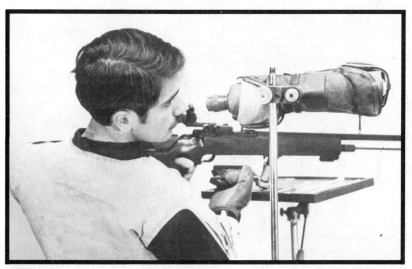

Equipment, including the spotting scope, should be conveniently located so the shooter can check his target without moving from his position.

The standard rifle is fired from the same position as the free-rifle, but without a butt-hook or palm-rest. The front hand may support the rifle in a variety of ways, as shown here.

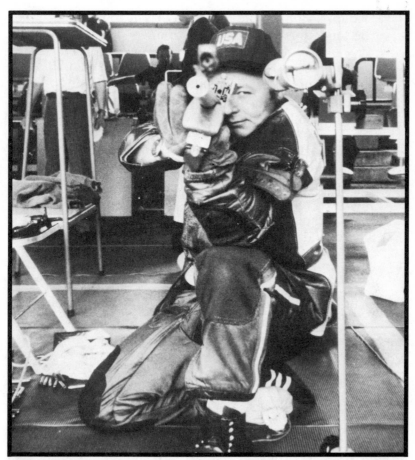

The foot should be placed on the kneeling roll without twisting; the shooter sits on the heel of his boot or shoe.

Kneeling position

1. The shooter should place the right knee on the shooting mat and a kneeling roll under the front of the right foot. The size and thickness of the kneeling roll depends upon the choice of the indi-

vidual as long as its legal. The right foot cannot be angled greater than 45° to one side,

2. In the erect position, the shooter places about 70 percent of his weight on the kneeling roll by sitting on the heel of his right foot. The spine and head remain erect.

3. In the forward position, the shooter places 60 to 70 percent of his weight on his left foot. The spine is curved forward and the head tilted slightly forward.

    The choice of an erect or forward position is an individual matter. Most shooters have a distinct preference, finding one more comfortable and stable than the other.

4. The left elbow rests comfortably on the left knee and supports the weight of the gun with the

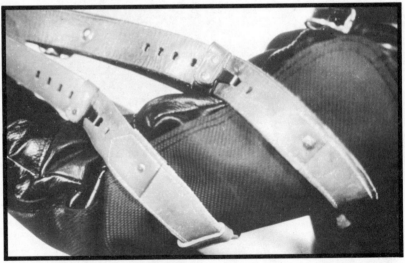

The sling may be placed high or low on the arm; it should not be placed midway, where it picks up the heaviest pulsebeat.

Two different shooters in the kneeling position. Note that one places most weight on the kneeling roll (erect position), other places more weight on the forward foot (forward position). Either position is acceptable.

bones of the forearm. The forearm is addition-
ally supported by a sling attached either high or
low on the upper left arm. The sling should not
be attached to the middle of the upper arm, as
this placement transmits a heavy pulse-beat to
the gun from the brachial artery in the back of
the arm.

5. The left hand should rest against the fore-end
   stop and support the rifle comfortably on the
   palm. A padded leather shooting glove is usually
   worn. The left hand does not grip the rifle.

6. The left thigh usually points slightly to the left
   of the target; the lower left leg is approximately
   vertical; the left toes may be pointed comfortably to the right of the position to gain added
   stability in the left-leg support structure.

7. The right arm pulls the gun back against the
   shoulder if a standard rifle is used. If a free-rifle
   is used, the butt hook may perform some of this
   work. The right hand grips the rifle in such a way
   that trigger pull does not disturb the aim of the
   gun.

Prone position

1. The shooter lies facing about 5 to 15 degrees to
   the right of the target. The body should be comfortably extended, with the spine and back muscles straight and relaxed.

2. The left leg remains relatively parallel to the
   spine. The left toes may be pointed inward, with
   the heel allowed to fall comfortably outward.

The left leg is usually parallel to the spine; the right leg may assume any position that is comfortable and stable.

3. The right leg may be placed in almost any position that is comfortable and stable. Usually the right knee is bent to some degree and the right toes point outward. The degree of leg angle and knee bend is largely a matter of individual choice. The degree that gives the best comfort and stability should be used.

4. The left elbow should be slightly to the left of the rifle. The left forearm is supported by a sling attached either high or low on the upper arm. The left hand should rest against the fore-end stop. Normally, a padded leather glove is worn. The rifle rests comfortably on the palm of the open hand. The fingers do not grip the rifle.

Details of two shooters in the prone position. The forward hand is high enough to meet legal requirements, but not so high that the position is uncomfortable or unstable.

5. The right elbow rests against the ground at a comfortable position and the right hand grips the rifle in such a way as to provide additional stability and a trigger pull that does not disturb the aim of the gun. The muscles controlling the right hand should be free of tension.

6. The position should be high enough to be legal and allow the eye to look through the sights without interference from the brow. But the position should not be so high that it becomes unstable or places a strain upon the neck, spine, or shoulders.

7. The right shoulder plays an important role in stabilizing the gun, especially during recoil, and the placement of the butt plate against the shoulder must be perfectly consistent each time the gun is fired. The butt plate may rest close to the neck against the collar bone, or further out against the muscles of the shoulder.

Comfort in rifle shooting usually requires some initial conditioning. In the standing position, the back-bend and twist may cause sore back muscles during the first few sessions. The kneeling position may cause initial discomfort in the right ankle, right knee, or sling arm. The prone position may initially cause slight soreness or bruising in the sling arm or right shoulder and sometimes a slightly stiff neck. With time, the body normally becomes conditioned to these stresses and the discomforts disappear. If you experience very sharp pain, or pain that does not diminish with time, examine your positions for excessive pressure, tightness, or stresses that may be the cause. If this procedure does not locate and eliminate the source of discomfort, consult a physician.

10
Training

Training is any effort directed toward increasing proficiency. Training can range from something as purely physical as a rigorous weight-lifting session to something as purely mental as reading or meditating, and anywhere in between. Training is a complex subject; its importance is reflected in the fact that this is the longest chapter in this book.

Competitive shooting sports are comparable to most other competitive sports today in regard to training. The most thoroughly trained individuals are the ones who win. In a sense, the image we have of an athlete beginning his activities at the start of a sporting event, continuing through to the finish, and emerging as the victor, is a deceptive or at least misleading image. Generally speaking, athletes do not "win" events, except in a technical sense, during the time-frame of the events themselves. They "win" in the training time they put in before the events—the hours, days, weeks, months, even years and decades of devoted efforts toward increasing their proficiency.

True, luck is occasionally involved, and whenever two athletes or two teams of equal ability and training confront each other, the outcome often hinges on chance, or "the breaks." But most athletes are familiar with the truth of the old saying, "The harder I work, the luckier I get." You, as a competitive marksman, need to confront this situation and come to terms with it in your own personal, unique way.

Our purpose in this chapter will not be to develop a training program for you. Only you can do that, for only you can determine your goals and set the standards of training that will enable you to reach those goals. What we will do here is discuss the principles, methods, and techniques of training that are known to be successful. As you will see, they are applicable not only to shooting sports, but to any competitive sport and even to life itself.

Ordinarily we would begin a discussion such as this with a definition. In fact, we already have: training is any effort directed toward increasing proficiency. The problem with this definition is that it is so broad and general that it can mean almost anything, and consequently it runs the risk of meaning nothing specifically. However, the breadth of the definition illustrates the nature of the problem quite nicely: training is a complex, many-sided subject. Moreover, there are different levels of training, so that what constitutes an effective training effort for a marksman at one level of development would be totally ineffective for a marksman at another level.

For example, a beginning marksman will train most effectively by directing about 95 percent of his efforts toward developing the physical components of position structure and motor skills. By contrast, a world-class marksman might train most effectively by devoting about 95 percent of his efforts toward developing the psychological components of mental discipline and a winning attitude. For either of these athletes to adopt the training schedule of the other would be utterly useless.

There are certain principles that underlie all training efforts, however, and although they are generally well known, it is worthwhile to review them in order to formulate realistic expectations about training.

One basic principle is that individuals come to each sport with unique ability levels. Simple observation tells us that when a group of people try a certain activity for the first time, some are more skillful than others. Why this is true is not always clear. Sometimes a skillful individual may be applying skills that he learned in other activities through a method called transference. In other instances, the skillful person may possess an innate talent or ability. But whatever the reason, there is little that can be done about this condition at the present state of our knowledge. It is, however, useful to recognize the existence of different ability levels because a beginner with a clear talent for marksmanship possesses one major component for potential future development. Innate talent alone, however, does not insure future success; other components, often broadly termed "character," play equally if not more important roles.

A second basic principle is that people learn at different rates. This can be true of physical as well as mental skills. Some people can learn physical skills quite rapidly; others are quick mentally; still others may be either quick or slow in both areas. The increased proficiency that accrues from learning efforts, or practice, is often called *training effect*, and individuals vary in the rate at which they exhibit training effects.

The training effect will be most pronounced when the athlete follows a training schedule that is optimal for him or her. Probably because of physical, physiological, and psychological variations among people, the optimal training schedule varies widely from individual to individual. What is best for one athlete is not necessarily best for another.

A training schedule will ordinarily be organized around daily blocks of training times, or sessions. The sessions can be varied according to duration, intensity, and frequency. In a shooter's training schedule, the duration of live-firing sessions may vary from a portion of an hour to several hours. The intensity of each session is largely a subjective factor and refers to how hard the shooter "works," physically and mentally, on improving performance. Intensity is not at all to be confused with speed, or rapidity of firing. Frequency refers to the rate at which sessions occur. One shooter might have one live-firing session each day; another might have one session every other day; and so on.

You as an individual are almost entirely responsible for determining your own optimal training schedule, for the basis of judgment is heavily subjective (although an intelligent and gifted coach can often be helpful). Each session should produce at least some progress. This is not always to be measured as a positive increase in performance. Some sessions—but certainly not all—may be devoted to experimenting with some physical or psychological change, only to result in an evaluation that the change is neutral or even negative. This, however, is a form of progress, for you learn what does not work. The most productive training sessions, though, are ones that produce positive increases in performance, and you should strive for a high percentage of positive sessions.

Somewhere within the range of extremely light and extremely heavy training schedules is your own optimal schedule. The ideal is to avoid undertraining, or too light a load, and overtraining, or too heavy a load. Undertraining does not allow full development of the potential training effect; overtraining produces diminishing returns for the efforts expended and, worse, introduces bad habits arising from physical or psychological fatigue; severe overtraining results in loss of interest and deep exhaustion.

We are reluctant to say precisely what an optimal training schedule should be, because the requirements vary widely among individuals and also with the practical necessities of the individual's life circumstances. Generally, experience and research indicate that a schedule is most productive when it consists of one session of an hour or more in duration each day, with an occasional day of rest once or twice a week. Some people can profit from two live-firing sessions a day, one in the morning and one in the late afternoon or evening, but this is not a practicable schedule for most people who have other obligations and interests. A frequency of less than one session a day tends to retard the training effect. Infrequently or erratically scheduled marathon sessions are almost always non-productive. In other words, it is better to train one hour a day five days a week, than five hours a day one day a week.

As you think about and experiment with developing your own optimal training schedule, you have to be realistic and practical. How many hours do you actually have available for training? Are there any other activities you could eliminate or perform more efficiently in order to make more training time available? Are you scheduling yourself too tightly, so that you have to rush constantly and feel harried? Are you getting enough sleep, rest, and recreation, and meeting your personal and family obligations? What is the quality of your training time? Are you coming to each session feeling strong and ready to concentrate, or are you tired or distracted by other worries so that the intensity of the sessions is very low? Only you can weigh all these considerations and devise a schedule that will be best for you.

It is psychologically damaging to devise an unrealistically ambitious schedule that you cannot follow; the results are discouragement, frustration, anger, and loss of interest. Devise a schedule that you can follow comfortably, and then stick to it, with realistic allowance for emergencies or circumstances that will require you to miss a session now and then. Of course, as you train more and more seriously and become more and more devoted to achieving your maximum potential, you will be willing to sacrifice in other areas of your life in order to follow your own ideal schedule without interruption or distraction.

In evaluating your schedule you should also be aware of what is popularly known as the *learning curve*. Proficiency acquisition takes place on an upward-tending curve interrupted by plateaus, which can be graphed as follows:

Over time, spurts of rapid learning are followed by periods in which little progress is apparent. The periods of rapid learning do not necessarily follow one another with the ordered frequency shown on the graph—they may be eratically spaced through time. The point, however, is that you should not assume that your training efforts are at fault whenever you find yourself on a plateau. If you're following a regular, well-planned schedule and find yourself stuck on a plateau for more than three weeks, though, it's time to undertake a re-evaluation. Sometimes you can get "unstuck" by taking a break for a couple of days and doing

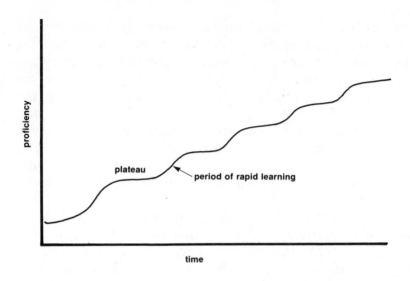

something completely different and recreational; or you might try a particularly long and arduous session in which you push yourself exceptionally hard to, but not much beyond, the point of fatigue. If neither of these methods works, begin looking for underlying causes in your training schedule or methods.

Let's summarize the main points of this chapter so far:

1. Proper training is necessary to winning at almost all levels of competition.

2. Training is many-sided, with both physical and psychological components.

3. Each person begins a sport with unique ability levels.

4. Each person learns at his or her own individual rate.

5. The rate of learning, or training effect, is directly related to the duration, intensity, and frequency of training sessions. The optimal schedule produces the greatest training effect.

6. You are the best judge of the effectiveness of your training schedule, but an intelligent coach can help. You should avoid undertraining or overtraining, and your schedule must be realistic.

7. Learning follows an upward curve through time, with alternating plateaus and periods of rapid learning.

These broad principles apply to both physical and psychological training, which overlap heavily. For ease of discussion we shall separate them, but as a thoughtful reader you will see that this separation is somewhat artificial.

Physical training—general

Physical training can be discussed within two parameters —specific and general. Specific training involves performing activities used in a particular sport. In other words, specific training for marksmanship is practice in shooting. General training, on the other hand, involves performing any activities that contribute to over-all physical fitness. We'll briefly discuss general training first.

Researchers have identified six major components of physical fitness: muscular strength, muscular endurance, flexibility, cardiorespiratory endurance, neuromuscular coordination, and reaction time. The first five can be enhanced by the following conditioning methods.

1. Muscular strength. Enhancement attained by progressive resistance exercises, such as selecting a heavy weight that can be lifted 5–10 times with maximum effort, then gradually increasing the weight in subsequent sessions while maintaining the same number of repetitions. Sources of information: physical fitness books; YMCA; health clubs; conditioning classes.

2. Muscular endurance. Enhancement attained by progressively increased repetitions of the same exercise, such as selecting a light or moderate weight that can be lifted 10–20 times with maximum effort, then gradually increasing the repetitions in subsequent sessions while retaining the same weight. Common sources of information: physical fitness books; YMCA; health clubs; conditioning classes.

3. Flexibility. Enhancement attained by progressive stretching exercises; static (motionless) stretching recommended over ballistic (bouncing or lunging) stretching; most commonly, exercises such as those found in Hatha yoga routines. Sources of information: physical fitness and yoga exercise books; some YMCA's; some health clubs; Hatha yoga classes.

4. Cardiorespiratory endurance. Enhancement attained by progressive exercise routines that sustain elevated heart and breathing rates; most commonly, jogging, swimming, biking. Sources of information: physical fitness and jogging books; YMCA; health clubs; conditioning classes.

5. Neuromuscular coordination. Enhancement attained to some degree by almost any activity requiring eye-hand or voluntary muscle coordination; enhancement tends to be specific to the activity rather than general. Neuromuscular coordination, while often dramatically improvable, seems more severely limited by innate factors than the previously identified components. Sources of information: specialized books;

conditioning classes; instruction and participation in a variety of sports activities.

6. Reaction time. Fast reaction time is commonly known as "quick reflexes." There are two components: stimulus-recognition time, such as determining the path of a tennis ball; and reflex time, in this case, swinging the racquet to return the ball. Stimulus-recognition time can be improved to some extent by training; reflex time appears to be innately fixed and little can be done to enhance this component in normal persons. Individuals with slow reaction times might expect to perform best in slow-fire marksmanship events rather than in rapid-fire or moving-target events that demand fast reaction times.

The value of a program of general fitness training to enhance marksmanship training is at present controversial and unclear. In an article published in the *UIT Journal,* September 1974, Drs. Porsch and Sovinz report on a research project in Austria in which the effect of heart rate was measured among elite pistol shooters. They conclude that a slow heart rate is beneficial. If their findings are correct, then cardiorespiratory endurance training would have value, for this lowers the resting heart rate by effectively increasing the stroke-volume of blood delivery.

On the other hand, Dr. Walter Bauer of Germany in the *UIT Journal,* July 1976, concludes that "a good shot is not dependent upon a slow pulse rate" and that "strenuous physical training is of no value to a shooter," though he does not conclude that it should be avoided.

A preliminary, multiple-authored report (unpublished) issued by the Motor Behavior Laboratory of the College of Health, Physical Education and Recreation of the Pennsylvania State University, however, confirms that elite pistol shooters tend to have better than average muscle strength and a history of active exercise; but the report concludes that body strength is not a critical factor in rifle shooting. Another unpublished report by Marie Alkerie using data from the

Penn State evaluation concludes, interestingly, that "the major factors in a successful shooting performance are high self esteem and mental preparedness."

There is, of course, much more data available, but this gives an overview of the conflicting opinions arising from the relevant research. What can we conclude?

First, we must recognize that we still do not know all we need to know about the role of general physical fitness in shooting sports. Investigations in this area are far behind those in other sports such as football, track, etc. This is an area in which future research could be quite valuable.

Second, we conclude from our own prolonged observations of elite marksmen's lifestyles that general fitness training appears to be of specific marksmanship value to some shooters, but not to others. Whether this is related to physical or psychological needs is not clear. It may well be that a high fitness level contributes significantly to some individuals' sense of self-esteem and preparedness, in which case it would contribute positively to confidence and a winning attitude.

Third, we know of no evidence so far that demonstrates that sensible general fitness training, properly scheduled, is detrimental to shooting performance.

Recommendations

The foregoing discussion would seem to indicate that for some people, general fitness training has no value. But this is not the complete picture. Volumes of data indicate the value of fitness programs in preventing degenerative diseases such as elevated serum cholesterol, arterio-sclerosis, other stress-related diseases, endomorphism (high body fat), and a host of other conditions.

Regular exercise is recommended by the American Medical Association, the American Heart Association, the President's Council of Physical Fitness, and numerous eminent health authorities. A *sensible* general fitness program, combined with sound nutrition, adequate sleep, and appropriate rest and relaxation, contributes to both physical and psychological health. We therefore recommend a program of exercise and general fitness training for every healthy adult. Whether such a general program will contribute positively to your marksmanship training in particular, however, is an individual matter which only you can determine.

Physical training—specific

Your body must make specific adaptations to the activities in marksmanship, and these adaptations are most effectively made by actually engaging in shooting, either by live-firing or by dry-firing. Here is one set of basic adaptations:

1. Your muscles must be conditioned to bearing the weight of the gun.

2. Your muscles must be conditioned to holding your body still in a firing position (and to tracking the target in moving-target events).

3. Your body must be conditioned to absorb the shock of recoil and the pressures of a sling, fore-end stop, butt plate, etc., if these are used.

These adaptations are quite specific and are a function of the duration and frequency of your training sessions. If you're a beginner or starting afresh after a prolonged layoff, you'll probably experience mild soreness in the muscles (and possibly joints) involved for a few days unless you begin with short, easy sessions. This is in fact a good way to begin. With daily practice, your body will gradually become conditioned to the stresses of aiming and firing a gun and the soreness will disappear. If soreness persists more than a couple of weeks, something is wrong. Look for an underlying cause and try to correct it before continuing.

In these areas, you should employ the technique of moderately overtraining for competitive events. For example, if the competition you enter requires you to fire 40 shots standing, train until you can comfortably fire 50 shots without undue fatigue. How do you do this? When you begin training, you may be able to shoot only 10 shots comfortably. Gradually increase the number through successive training sessions until you can do 50; then you'll be able to shoot your 40 with a reserve of strength and energy to carry you through the string in top form. If you train to fire only 40 shots, you're likely to suffer damaging fatigue under the additional stresses of competition and exhibit decreased performance toward the end of the string.

Here's another set of adaptations.

1. Your muscles must be trained to hold your body motionless.

2. The muscles controlling your trigger finger must be trained to pull the trigger smoothly in isolation from all other muscles.

These adaptation, you'll recall, coincide precisely with the second fundamental of shooting. Both adaptations are made progressively and are a function of training time and effort. We believe that progress in both functions can be rapid on occasion, but that no one ever reaches maximum potential in either area. No matter how proficient you become in either, there will still be room for improvement if you work at it.

You may find that progress in these functions is sometimes erratic, even reversible. On certain days you will seem to lose all stability and steadiness; or there may be days when your trigger pull seems jerky and uncoordinated. Expect these days—they are normal. The best way to overcome them is probably by dry-firing with particular emphasis on controlling the relevant muscles.

While we're on this subject, we should mention that dry-firing is an excellent way to train in both these areas. It is much less troublesome because it can be practiced in your living room or bedroom with a reduced target, or with a normal target reflected in a series of mirrors to approximate actual firing distances. And of course dry-firing eliminates the cost of ammunition. Dry-firing is a regular training technique for almost all serious marksmen.

You can also use dry-firing as well as live-firing sessions to accomplish two other training goals—increased autonomic control of breathing and heart rates. The autonomic system is the part of the central nervous system that regulates certain "automatic" body functions without conscious direction.

Marksmanship requires breathing techniques that initially must be regulated consciously, but with practice the autonomic system will control them more-or-less automatically, leaving you free to focus your attention on other functions. In rapid-fire or moving-target events, you would probably inhale a moderate amount, then simply hold your breath while firing. In slow-fire events, however, the correct breathing technique looks like this on a graph:

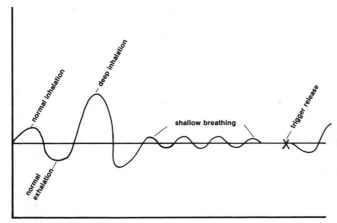

As you begin aiming, you take a deep breath followed by a slightly greater-than-normal exhalation, another normal inhalation, and then continue with increasingly shallow breathing that finally ceases a few moments before firing.

With continued practice, this will become so natural that you will hardly ever be aware of it.

Also with practice, you'll acquire the capacity to slow your heart (pulse) rate while aiming and firing. On a graph, the rate looks like this:

Normally in competition a shooter's heart rate is quite rapid just before firing the first shot in a string. If the shot is a good one, the person's heart rate will tend to decrease; if it is a bad shot, heart rate will increase. Increases also occur at other points of special importance, such as after shooting a 6, or toward the end of an unusually long string of 10's, or just before the final shot in a string. Shooters who worry about their scores or experience anxiety during a match will tend to have elevated heart rates. Shooters who remain detached and calm experience less pulse-rate elevation.

Studies at Penn State seem to show that heart rate has little effect on pistol shooters, but considerable effect upon rifle shooters. The reason is simple. When you're holding a rifle, numerous points of body contact transmit minute but significant pulses to the gun. You can readily observe this by attaching a target scope to the rifle. Each time your heart beats, the scope will show a corresponding slight upward jump. The proper technique in rifle shooting is to time the trigger release so that it does not occur immediately before, after, or during the pulse, but during the interval of steadiness between beats. The slower your pulse rate, the greater the length of the steady interval, and the better your chances of timing the release correctly.

You don't really have to make an effort to train your heart to slow down as you prepare to release a rifle shot. With time and practice, it begins to happen as the autonomic system develops the capacity. You can help the process somewhat through cardiorespiratory endurance training, which slows the resting pulse rate, and possibly also by practicing meditation, about which we'll say more later.

The progression of physical training

A beginner will of necessity be preoccupied with position building, with designing a position structure that provides a stable support to the gun. He will also be concerned with developing control of the support muscles that hold the body still, and with developing a smooth trigger pull. In the first several training sessions, at least, he will experience a great deal of instability and erratic muscle control. Shots may range from the 10-ring to the 6-ring, and occasionally completely out into the white. The subjective sensation is often described as a feeling of clumsiness and an uncertainty about how to identify and correct problems. The beginner will almost be forced to experiment with more-or-less random changes and to use a certain amount of guesswork in attempting to refine the position structure.

As the training effect develops and control is gained over support and trigger-pull muscles, the feeling of clumsiness and uncertainty begins to dissipate. With more control over muscles, imperfections in the position structure can be subjectively sensed and identified, and specific corrections can be attempted, often with success. As this stage develops, randomness and guesswork can gradually be eliminated from the position building process and a scientific method can be employed.

From the beginning, dry-firing sessions are more valuable

than live-firing sessions in producing a useful training effect. Most beginners, of course, understandably wish to fire live rounds, to "see what I can do." But live firing at this stage tends to focus attention on score rather than on position structure and muscle control. Dry-firing enables the shooter to keep attention on his body as he aims and pulls the trigger. Through this process he can more rapidly develop his kinesthetic sense, or awareness of body position and muscles functions, and the result is more rapid progress in position building and in refining muscle control.

We have mentioned that a shooter should keep a diary. In the diary he should begin recording his growing kinesthetic awareness, describing in detail, and as completely as possible, the various kinesthetic sensations he experiences and what measures he takes to refine muscle control (in addition to structural changes in the position). The necessity of writing down in clear language the sensations he experiences is a means of clarifying his own understanding of his body and bringing his sometimes subliminal awareness into clear, conscious focus. We cannot overemphasize the value of such a diary. It is perhaps the most valuable tool available to a shooter, at any stage of development, to speed up progress.

As the shooter continues to develop, he will move toward increasingly smaller refinements in position structure and body control until, perhaps, he reaches the championship stage. Even at these advanced stages, the diary will continue to be of great value.

Now for some general principles to consider in the physical training sequence.

1. Train in only one position or gun at a time until reasonable mastery is attained.

   In three-position rifle training, for example, train initially in only one position; in pistol training, work with only one gun. The reason is that if you try to work with two positions or guns at the same time, you will not make very rapid progress in either because your mental and physical efforts will be divided. Master one set of functions first; then reduce your practice time in the first set of functions to about 20 percent of each training session, and devote 80 percent to the new, second set of problems. When you've gained reasonable mastery over the second position or gun, you can divide the time in your training sessions any way you think is best to enhance your progress.

2. Begin training first in the most difficult position or event.

At this point its about time we flew in the face of tradition. For many years we began our junior shooting in the prone position. This in the belief that it is the easiest and safest for the beginner. We believe that now there is sufficient evidence to support a different method of teaching. So we would like to offer for your consideration the idea that all rifle shooting should begin from the standing position. We think there are several valid reasons to support us.

Number one, remember the first time someone put a sling on you, and strapped you into the rifle? Not at all easy nor comfortable. And we don't feel it's any safer than the standing position.

Number two, the most natural way for anyone, novice or expert, to hold a rifle is in the standing position. Watch people pick up a rifle to "feel" or examine it. They always place the rifle in the shoulder to see how it points. It seems to be the natural thing to do.

Number three, when our junior or novice begins to progress to a lower position, it is more stable, and his score will quickly improve. Conversely, if our budding champion is going from prone to a higher position, the new position will be less stable and progress will be slower.

Number four, the air rifle program supports the theory fully of beginning to shoot from the standing position. There are literally thousands upon thousands of beginning shooters that are quite proficient shooting standing and have never fired any of the other positions.

If you follow these principles in your training program, we believe your rate of progress will be much faster than that of someone whose program is organized differently.

Psychological training

As we've just seen, the beginning shooter will of necessity not be concerned with psychological training. But as training progresses, psychological training becomes the principal factor that separates the winners from the also-rans. Psychological training is the "secret" of all gold medal winners.

Psychological training is essential in laying four foundation-stones for a successful marksmanship training program. They are 1) a training plan to reach a specific goal; 2) proper mental function while aiming and firing; 3) proper self-control during competition; and 4) training to be a winner. Goal-formation is basic to the other three. Initially it does not seem to be a psychological training function, but upon further consideration it emerges as indispensible to proper psychological training.

Goal formation.

No one else should attempt to determine what your goals are; ultimately, only you can do that. And you cannot determine what your shooting goals can be until you've had enough experience to make a realistic assessment of your talent, ambition, and life circumstances. But sooner or later, if you want to be a winner at any level, you will have to formulate training goals if you're to be successful.

Your goal can be anything you want it to be. It may be something as simple as shooting a higher score than your neighbor Charlie, or it may be an Olympic gold medal or even

Your goal can be anything you want it to be, from beating your neighbor in friendly competition to a distinguished national medal to a series of Olympic gold medals.

a series of Olympic gold medals. The level of competition is not important. If you set a specific goal and attain it, you're successful; if you don't reach it, you've failed.

Goal formulation is just as important in living as it is in shooting. Without goals, we're like a ship on the open seas without a compass or a sextant. We can head this way or that without any idea of where we're going. We usually end up going in circles, or arriving at some destination that we didn't really want.

Goals are essentially dreams. To establish a goal, you have to ask yourself, "What do I want from my life?" The answer is usually an achievement of some kind. Pin it down to something specific, and you have a goal. If you have a real desire to reach it, if you *want* the goal, you have motivation. If real motivation is lacking, setting the goal is rather useless. Motivation is the engine that drives the ship to its destination.

A goal should be interesting and realistic. It will be interesting only if it offers enough difficulty to pose a real challenge, to tax your wits and abilities. If it's too easy, it's probably not very interesting. But if it's too difficult, or just plain unreachable, it's unrealistic. There's no point in attempting the impossible. But remember this: a goal, a dream, can often enable you to do things far beyond what you could do without it. All of us admire people who dare to dream of great things and then accomplish them.

A difficult goal, one that requires a great deal of effort, is attainable only if it is consistent with your life values. For example, if you set a goal of winning a gold medal as an Olympic rifleman, but find that achievement in sports and particularly in shooting is not really important in your overall system of values, then chances are you will not reach that goal. Difficult goals sometimes require almost all of your time and energies, a kind of life effort. You cannot have a divided system of values and expect to reach such goals. The difficult goal demands careful organization, careful expenditure of energies, and numerous compromises and sacrifices in other areas of your life. In exchange, achieving the goal offers very high levels of self-esteem and personal gratification.

It must be remembered, though, that achieving any goal, no matter how lofty, does not guarantee or even offer lasting happiness. How many times have you thought, "If only I owned one of these, or accomplished this, then I'd be happy and satisfied." But after you owned or accomplished what you wanted, you weren't really happy except for a brief time. Soon you became restless and dissatisfied until you found something else you wanted and could work for. Satisfaction comes not from attaining a goal (though there is a brief feeling of happiness), but from progressing toward the goal. Success, really, is not a place; it is a journey.

For this reason, goals in life need periodic reassessment. When we reach one goal, or find that we can make no further progress toward a goal, it is time to set new goals, develop new dreams that we can work toward. Without these dreams, we are adrift and going nowhere.

All right. Let's talk about you as a marksman. You have your goal. You're motivated. The goal is interesting and realistic and consistent with your life values. You have a fairly good idea of the rewards you'll derive from reaching the goal. Now what?

Here's what you do. You formulate a plan; you map out a route that will take you to your destination. You envision specific ports of call along the way. The goal is your ultimate destination, the *long range goal*. The intermediate ports of call are the *short range goals* that will get you there.

For example, let's say that your goal is to fire a score of at least 1180 in 3-position ISU rifle competition. You're presently capable of firing practice scores of 1050: 320 in standing, 350 in kneeling; and 380 in prone. With a bit of quick figuring, you realize that you'll have to be able to fire 385 or better in standing, 397 or better in kneeling; and 398 or better in prone. After assessing your potential for progress and the training time available to you, you decide that you can reach these scores in about 24 months. So you set specific goals for progress in each of the three positions. In the first six months, you'll concentrate heavily on your standing position with the goal of raising your scores to an average of at least 385 by that time. This is the first short range goal.

Then you'll devote the next six months to maintaining your standing performance and raising your kneeling scores to an average of at least 397. This is the second short range goal. Then you'll spend the next six months maintaining standing and kneeling performance and raising your prone scores to an average of at least 398. This is the third short range goal.

Then, in the final six months, you'll concentrate on putting together your performance in all three positions for an average aggregate score of at least 1180, your long range goal.

Notice that in each case, we specified goals of *at least* 385, 397, and 398. This is an important specification. It means that the goal is formulated for a minimum performance, with no limits beyond. If you formulate a goal as a maximum performance, you automatically impose psychological barriers against further improvement. Always formulate minimum or "at least" shooting goals.

Now you do a couple of things of great importance, things that, if you're unfamiliar with these techniques, may seem a bit strange; but we assure you that these techniques have worked very well for many people.

First, write down your long and short range goals in a brief list, including dates. Make several copies, and carry one in your wallet. Put the other copies where you will see them daily. Put one on the mirror in your bathroom, one in with your shooting equipment, one on the refrigerator door, one on your bedside table. Form the habit of reading these and concentrating on the goals every time you see one of the lists. In idle moments, take the list from your wallet, read it, and concentrate on it. Read the list on your bedside table before you go to sleep at night and concentrate on it as you fall asleep.

Second, in your concentration on these goals, visualize yourself accomplishing each of them. See yourself actually meeting or exceeding each one.

Your purpose here is to imbue your mind, consciously and subconsciously, with an absolute certainty that these are your goals and that you can reach them. You want to be completely positive in this effort, so that you eliminate any doubts that imply "If I reach these goals" and establish a rock-solid conviction that says "I will reach these goals."

These simple techniques clarify your values and build your faith in yourself in ways you may not believe until you've given them an honest try. Do not expect results overnight, however. You may have to use the technique regularly for several months for it to be effective.

At the same time that you formulate your goals, you should devise and write a training plan. It too should be in a physical form, something you can look at and read. And you should read it frequently.

It should include a calendar on which you indicate each training session along with the dates on which you will accomplish each goal. For example, suppose you choose to train for two hours a day on weekdays, and four hours on Saturdays and alternate Sunday afternoons. You may actually plan a more- or less-rigorous schedule, but whatever it is, write it down, indicating specific times and days.

Then you try to follow your schedule as closely as possible. Occasionally, circumstances will require you to miss a session. Try to make it up somewhere. You will find that from time to time you will be tempted by other attractions. Ignore them. You will also find that on certain days or weeks, you will feel a lazy aversion to training, a feeling of "I just don't want to." The best solution is to make yourself get started, to make yourself go to the range and set up your equipment. Once you begin working, interest will usually reappear. If you find yourself permanently caught in a reluctance to train, you're either overtraining, physically ill, or experiencing some conflict in your values or your personal life. In the latter case, a thorough reassessment of your goals is required.

Finally, your training plan should also include a certain number of competitive events. You need to shoot in a few matches to break the monotony of training, to test your methods, and to acclimatize yourself to the pressures of competition. Some people like to shoot about 12 to 15 matches per year, spaced at about one a month, or even more; others feel satisfied with 3 or 4 matches a year. Only you can determine what's right for you, but 6 to 8 matches a year seems about average.

As you work toward a long range goal, the matches you shoot along the way should be regarded as training events. Naturally, you try to perform the best you can, but you do not attempt to unnaturally intensify your physical training or focus your psychological training on one of these events in order to bring yourself to a training peak. In the hypothetical example in which we set your goal as an 1180 in 24 months, you would attempt to peak for one important match at the end of that period, an effort that would confirm and fulfil your entire long range effort. But you would not peak for the intermediate matches, as this would interrupt your steady training march toward the final goal.

Now let's review.

1. Establish a specific long range goal and specific short range goals.

2. Write the goals down and review them frequently.

3. Develop absolute faith in your ability to achieve the goals.

4. Write a specific training schedule and follow it.

5. Enter a reasonable number of matches but do not make an effort to peak until you approach your final goal.

Proper mental function while aiming and firing

Earlier in the book we described the non-verbal state of consciousness during aiming and firing, a state brought about quite probably by engaging the right hemisphere of the brain in concepts of spatial relationships and fine motor control.

Beginning shooters will have difficulty doing this at first, largely because in Western culture we are strongly conditioned to verbal thinking. But with practice and effort, the proper non-verbal mode of consciousness becomes easier and easier. So perhaps the most direct way of training for the proper psychological state is through repeated efforts while aiming and firing in training sessions, particularly dry-firing sessions. Ideally, you want to completely eliminate verbal thought while aiming and firing.

Since this psychological state seems to bear some relationship to the alpha state, indicated by a recognizable pattern of brain waves on an oscilloscope, there is possibly a transference value to be gained from additional experience in putting yourself into the state of deep relaxation associated with alpha waves. There are numerous techniques for doing this. One is through the use of bio-feedback equipment which electronically monitors brain waves and provides a signal when alpha waves are produced.

Other ways involve various techniques of deep meditation which can be attained by practicing Transcendental Meditation, mental yoga, or other disciplines. A respectable book on this subject is *The Relaxation Response* by Dr. Howard Benson of the Harvard University Medical School. By experimenting with several of the techniques, you may find one that works best for you. While the general health value of deep relaxation in dealing with stress is widely acknowledged, at this time it is unclear whether practicing the techniques has any positive transference value for marksmanship. We would appreciate a letter from anyone who gains insight into this subject through personal experience. A clear value of meditation techniques, however, is that they enable the practitioner to relax and clear his mind during training and competition.

Another unquestionably useful technique is that of mental rehearsal, also sometimes called imaging or conceptualization. The technique involves closing your eyes and creating a mental image of yourself in position, aiming, and firing a perfect shot with perfect follow-through. You attempt not only to see yourself shooting a 10, but to feel the kinesthetic sensations as well.

Mental rehearsal is now used by top athletes in almost every sport. It is probably safe to say that today, at the higher levels of all sports, it is an essential training technique, for it contributes to learning physical skills and to preparing for future performances of those skills.

As a marksman you should use the technique not only to reproduce the physical sensations of shooting, but also the non-verbal psychological state that should coincide with a perfect performance. The benefits of rehearsal are then both physical and mental.

There is a caveat to mental rehearsal, however. You should not use mental rehearsal until you have refined your physical techniques to a fairly advanced level. Apparently, mental rehearsal establishes or reinforces neural pathways that are used in actual performances, and thus contributes to habit formation. If you reinforce the pathways involved in incorrect performance, you are only strengthening bad habits. This is analogous to programming a computer with the wrong data or instructions; the computer output is consequently incorrect. Computer programmers characterize this as "garbage in, garbage out." Don't use mental rehearsal until you've learned the proper physical techniques of shooting; otherwise, you'll be programming your own "garbage in, garbage out."

Mental rehearsal can be practiced anywhere, any time. The optimal time, however, appears to be directly following a training session. After completing the session, relax for a few minutes and then mentally rehearse the experience of shooting perfect shots. Perform the rehearsal several times, as perfectly as possible. In this way, you reinforce the progress you made in actual training.

This technique is also useful in controlling the anxiety aroused by competition, which is our next topic.

Proper self-control during competition

When you enter competition, you experience a level of apprehension and anxiety about the outcome and about your own performance. Physically you feel nervous and tense; your heart rate goes up; you sweat at the armpits and palms; your stomach may feel uneasy. Mentally, you're distracted by all of these physical symptoms and your mind tends to race with questions about "How will I perform—well, or poorly?"

Collectively, all of this means that you have to exercise more self control in competition in order to meet or exceed your training performance. There are numerous techniques for achieving this form of self discipline, and most individuals eventually develop individualized coping patterns. Several concepts are widely agreed upon by experienced shooters, however, and can be summarized as follows.

1. Become familiar with competitive events. As a beginner, you'll find it useful to observe one or more events before you actually compete. After that, it is useful to enter matches on a regular schedule, say every one or two months, in order to become familiar with match routines and re-

quirements, and with your own feelings of anxiety aroused by the competitive situation. Unfamiliar circumstances or situations in themselves arouse anxiety; as you become more familiar with competitions, your anxiety abates.

2. Recognize that anxiety is your enemy only if you let it be. If you give yourself over to anxiety, you can become a nervous wreck, unable to do anything except embarrass yourself on the firing line. But you can choose to look at anxiety another way. For one thing, everyone in the competition is experiencing the same anxiety you are, because it is quite normal—so that evens everything out. For another, anxiety simply means that you are attaching a great deal of importance to the competition, and this in turn will make you more alert and finely tuned and can actually improve your performance. Instead of being frightened by anxiety, you can turn it into a positive advantage.

3. Develop a physical routine in training that you can duplicate in competition. Before competing, organize a few training sessions that are timed exactly like the match, and perform a kind of dress rehearsal in which you do everything just as you intend to do it in the match. Expect conditions in the match to be slightly different, but nevertheless concentrate on developing a routine for handling your equipment and a timing and pace that will work well in the competition. This will increase your self-assurance and allay anxieties that arise from feeling unprepared.

4. Develop a detached, objective attitude. In competition, there is a powerful temptation to wonder

and worry about how other competitors are doing. Forget the others. There is nothing you can do to affect their scores. If one of them beats you, he beats you; but it's not the end of the world. Similarly, be detached about your own problems. If you shoot an 8 through an error, or the wind blows your otherwise perfect shot into the 9-ring, simply accept it as a fact, without becoming emotional or worrying about it. What's done is done, and there's nothing to be gained by giving it another thought. The more detached and objective you become, the more you allay anxiety and avoid thought patterns that interfere with proper mental function. In competition, the perfect shooter controls his emotions and never worries.

This attitude should apply also to adverse conditions on the range, such as wind, rain, noise, interruptions or delays, and anything else that makes conditions less than ideal. Usually these conditions will affect everyone on the firing line. You can choose to be upset by them, or you can choose to be detached and to continue performing at full capacity.

5. Limit your thinking to positively planning the next shot or to solving match problems. Sometimes match conditions pose problems: the surface of your firing point may have an unusual slope, or the wind may be blowing erratically, or the target may be at an unaccustomed height. In situations like these, you have to cooly and rationally devise a solution. Actually, you should have anticipated most such problems and devised solutions prior to the match, during your pre-match inspection of the range (more about this later). But sometimes the unexpected oc-

curs, and you have to deal with it. Fine. Deal with it intelligently and decisively. But otherwise, limit your thinking to planning your next shot. Eliminate thoughts about your past mistakes or your future score. Think only of your next shot, not your next 2 or 10 shots, and think positively. Do not think "I must not shoot another 8." Instead, think "I will shoot a 10," and try to mentally see yourself doing just that. You will, in effect, be practicing mental rehearsal between shots, and the more effectively you can do this, the better the chances that your next shot will be a 10.

6. Be particularly careful of your health and training habits prior to a match. If you're serious about your shooting, you probably will not use alcohol or tobacco at all while you're in training, though many shooters feel that a moderate amount of alcohol in the evening (after training!) is not harmful. However, before a match, you will benefit from drinking no alcohol at all for several days and from avoiding any kind of drugs, even prescription drugs unless they are absolutely necessary. Your meals should be regular, nourishing, and not too filling. You should get your usual, amount of sleep. You want to feel rested, strong, healthy, fit and confident when you begin competing, with your body in peak condition.

7. Arrive at the match site early. A day or two in advance of the competition is not too early if you can afford the time. Most larger events will open the range for practice at least one day before competition begins. You can gain several advantages by an early arrival. Most obviously, per-

haps, is that you avoid rushing in at the last minute or even arriving too late to compete. Being pushed for time will not contribute to your mental and emotional equanimity. But just as important, you can become familiar with the surroundings and adjust yourself psychologically to the environment and the conditions. You can study the wind and light; you can examine the firing points, the targets, and other facilities that will affect your preparation; and you can anticipate any adjustments you might have to make to deal with the problems you may encounter. You can also meet and socialize with other competitors, range officials, and visitors, which will add pleasure to your visit.

Note: if a match will occur in unusual conditions, such as in a significantly different altitude or climate, you may wish to arrive a week or two before the match to acclimatize yourself and determine the effects on your equipment. Athletes who did not train at high altitudes before events in Mexico City, for example, were severely affected by the altitude and thin air at this city which is over a mile above sea level.

8. Spend the hours before the match in mental preparation. Normally, you will begin to feel anxiety as starting time approaches. Some people try to deal with this by devoting their attention to other things. They play cards or horseshoes or frisbee, they socialize, they go shopping. These activities certainly are not harmful and they do occupy the mind, but they do not make any positive contribution to preparation or performance.

Spend at least some of the hours before the match in positive mental preparation. You can begin by checking and organizing your equipment. Then you mentally put yourself through the routine you've developed for the match. Then you can mentally envision yourself in the match, watching yourself from the outside, as you shoot your sighting rounds, fire each string, and complete the match. Then practice mental rehearsal, feeling yourself in position and firing shot after shot into the 10-ring with perfect mental functioning. When the match finally begins, you'll feel more familiar and comfortable with your situation, and your confidence and your performance will be better.

If you wish to rest in the hours before the match, an excellent technique which refreshes the body and seems to sharpen the ability to concentrate is to practice meditation, or the deep relaxation methods, discussed in Dr. Howard Benson's book, *The Relaxation Response*. Not everyone can use these techniques; but if you can, it is one of the best possible ways to rid yourself of anxiety and its associated fatigue, and to bring yourself to a peak of mental and physical preparedness.

The same technique can also be used during a match when you feel fatigued or excessively keyed up. Meditation relieves the state of excitation in the muscular and nervous systems without leaving you with the feeling of being "let down." or overly relaxed.

9. Remember that chemical crutches always break down in competition. Some people attempt to deal with anxiety by resorting to psychological crutches—principally alcohol or drugs. These substances don't work. They may give the illu-

sion of a good performance, but it is only an illusion. Alcohol consumption interferes with vision, coordination, and judgment, and is positively dangerous in combination with firearm use. Many prescription and over-the-counter tranquilizers and stimulants—as well as drugs of any kind—adversely affect vision and coordination.

A recent exception is a class of drugs informally called beta-blockers. A detection test from blood or urine samples is currently being developed and the use of beta-blockers will be grounds for disqualification or worse, possibly by the time you read this.

Drugs have no place in athletic competition and are illegal by NRA and ISU rules. Athletic events are meant to test the performance of human beings, not chemicals. The use of drugs and other artificial crutches is a cowardly failure to confront the true challenge of sports, which is self-mastery. The key to self-mastery is training and only training. To use chemical crutches is to assault your own pride and self-esteem. Rely on training instead; you will never regret it.

Here, then, is a summary.

1. Become familiar with competitive events.

2. Recognize that anxiety is your enemy only if you let it be.

3. Develop a routine in training that you can duplicate in competition.

4. Develop a detached, objective attitude.

5. Limit your thinking to positively planning the next shot or to solving match problems.

6. Be particularly careful of your health and training habits prior to a match.

7. Arrive at the match site early.

8. Spend the hours before the match in mental preparation.

9. Remember that chemical crutches always break down in competition.

You may develop other techniques for self control in competition, but these are proven by experience and are known to be effective. If you employ these techniques, quite possibly they will be all you will need.

Training to be a winner

Thus far we have talked about training in terms of setting a personal performance goal—a certain aggregate score—and working to achieve it. If your training goals take your development high enough, you'll eventually find that, as you work toward meeting this goal in competition, you'll be in a position to win the event. Few people can confront the prospect of winning an event for the first time without suffering intense anxiety and self-doubt. Probably this is because the person who has no experience in winning has no self-image of himself as a winner to support his new role.

The effect of this anxiety and self doubt may cause a serious drop in performance because the individual "tries too hard." Here is where the experienced winner has an edge over the novice. The experienced shooter has a clear self-image of himself as a winner in competition and knows that if he just performs normally, his chances of winning are very good. Consequently his mental functions are the ones he is accustomed to using in training and competition, and he is usually successful in turning in a good performance. By contrast, the novice who finds himself in a position to win will often begin to "try harder" to insure success. As a consequence, his mental functions begin to differ from his normal pattern, he may begin to think verbally while aiming, and this interrupts his physical performance; his scores suffer. This pattern is likely to persist until the person develops a strong self-image of himself as a winner.

How do you develop the self-image of a winner? There are two basic approaches, one practical, and one psychological.

The practical approach is to enter—or even to schedule your own—competitive events against other competitors that you are almost certain to beat. Some people will of course scorn "easy" matches as being meaningless, but they are not. They give you the experience of winning and reinforce your self-image as a winner. Limited experience like this is especially good for every beginner.

Of course, you want to increase the level of competition as time goes by, so that your self-image is tested and reinforced by experience in difficult, more realistic competitions. We think it's useful for everyone to include a few easy matches in his or her training schedule each year, simply to reinforce the experience of winning. The opposite of this is to enter only competitions which are too difficult and give you no chance of winning. If you confine yourself exclusively to this type of event, you are only reinforcing you self-image as a loser, a questionable training procedure.

The other approach is psychological and not significantly different from the technique used in goal setting. You establish the goal of winning a specific event. Write the goal down and begin visualizing yourself as the winner. See yourself shooting the match, controlling anxiety, performing normally and smoothly. Then see your score posted on the announcement board in first place. Then see yourself accepting the winner's trophy. Rehearse these mental images and rehearse them and rehearse them until they completely permeate your conscious and subconscious minds. If you're a beginner, you should allow several months for this process to be effective. Experienced winners use this process for at least several weeks in training for a particular event.

Developing a positive self-image of yourself as a winner is something which you do privately, without discussing it freely with anyone not intimately involved in directing your training program. If you tell other people you are going to win a particular event, you introduce additional sources of anxiety, because if you lose, not only do you fall short of a personal goal, you also lose face by appearing to be a braggart who can't back up his boasts. This additional pressure can have a strong negative impact on your match performance.

As part of your psychological training, try to develop the attitude of a gracious winner. Avoid bragging and arrogance, for these actually undercut the basis of self confidence in yourself and make you rather objectionable to boot. A strong self-image of yourself as a winner should imbue you with quiet self confidence, an inner sense of calm and security that allows you to accept victory graciously and to be grateful for the fine efforts of your competitors, to regard their performances with genuine respect. You'll find that, as you become a proven and mature champion with much experience in winning, you'll even become interested in helping others improve their performances in order to better your own competition and spur yourself on to greater efforts. This itself is an admirable long range goal, but one that can be set only by an advanced competitor.

You should also learn how to handle losing in an acceptable fashion. If you're a true champion, you never expect to lose, you never even consider losing. But in every event there is only one winner, and this is usually the person with the most talent and/or the highest level of training. It will not always be you. Let's examine some myths about winning.

1. Anyone can win.

True only in a special sense. If you set a performance goal for yourself in competition—a certain score—and meet that goal, you are successful. You can regard yourself as a winner. But public recognition will go to the individual who took first place in the event. He may have won the event even though he fell short of his own personal performance goal. Then who is the real winner? It depends on how you define winning. We think people who realize their fullest potential at any stage of their shooting careers are winners. An Olympic shooter who wins a gold medal with a score short of his potential will win public acclaim, but is not as much of a winner as a paraplegic who shoots the best score of his life in a match arranged for wheel-chair victims.

2. If you work hard and do your best, you will win.

Depends on how you define your terms. Hard work will result in progress only if it is the right kind of work, performed efficiently. The wrong training effort will not produce a desired training effect. Further, doing your best means one thing if you interpret it to mean performing normally according to your training standards, another thing if it means "trying harder" during competition. As we've seen, "trying hard" can produce negative effects. But even if you train hard and effectively and perform at your best in a competition, you may still lose. You may come up against someone else who has trained harder and/or has more natural ability. Rarely, you'll lose to someone who gained an edge through good luck—better weather conditions during his relay, for example.

3. Winning is not everything; it is the only thing.

Often credited to the late Vince Lombardi, but he did not actually make this statement. Let's examine it very briefly.

What do you mean by winning? Taking first place in an event, or achieving your own performance goal? The two can be synonomous if you set your personal goal high enough. If your goal is a score that you know none of your competitors can beat, or if you're going for a new world record, then obviously you're going for first place in the event, too. In terms of your effort, taking first place becomes synonomous with your personal goal, the "only thing" you're striving for in training. Interpreted this way, the statement attributed to Lombardi makes sense. But not everyone needs to set goals high enough to insure first place in competition.

Your pleasure and satisfaction in shooting will be much greater if you maintain healthy perspectives about winning and losing. Set goals that are realistic. This does not mean that you should set "easy" goals. On the contrary, you should set them as high as you realistically can. Doing this requires self-knowledge and careful thought and planning, and usually much revision. If you honestly believe you are capable of a new world record, go for it. Set a personal performance goal, plan your training, and then do it. But if you're not capable of such heights of achievement—if you lack the talent or time or resources—setting such a goal is self defeating. Set a goal that is within your reach, work for it, and then enjoy the satisfaction of knowing that you made it.

If the goal you set happens to be one that you believe will win first place in an event, and you reach it but don't take first place, try not to become bitter or discouraged. Similarly, accept that sometimes match conditions or equipment failures will affect your performance. Resolve to win next time, to win by perseverance and further improvement, to win in spite of the obstacles posed by other competitors, range conditions, or equipment. Losers think "I can't win because of these obstacles." Winners think "I'll win next time in spite of these obstacles." Losers complain, make excuses, and wallow in disappointment and bitterness. Winners accept their position in an event, congratulate the winners, and begin planning for success next time.

Underlying this discussion of winning and losing, of course, is the issue of goal setting. Where will you set your

goals? What do you want from shooting, and from the over-
all scheme of your life? How important to you is achievement
in this sport? Do you want it to be only a hobby and pleasant
pastime? Or do you want to be your state champion? Do you
want a regional title? A national title? A world record?

As you move up the ladder of goals into the rarified atmosphere of world-class competition, the importance of talent
and the value of training and experience become increasingly
high. The demands of time and discipline are great. Years of
specialized effort must be put in to enable you to compete
against other world-class shooters who are also putting in
years of specialized effort.

The decision to move into the arena of world-class competition is one that should be based entirely upon an individual's
own motivations. It is essentially an adult decision, requiring
adult judgment and self-awareness. It is perhaps indicative
that the average age of world champion shooters is above
thirty. In shooting as in many other sports, we sometimes see
the sad spectacle of youngsters being pushed prematurely
by their parents into rigorous, demanding training programs. The ambitions derive from the parents, not the
youngsters, and the results are usually unfortunate, not only
because the youngsters eventually become soured on shooting sports, but also because the unnatural training schedule
forces him or her to develop one dimension of his personality
at the expense of all other dimensions by depriving him of the
normal range of teen-age experiences. Parents who push
their children toward championships in any sport run the risk
of burdening the child with grave personality and adjustment
problems.

But to some mature individuals, the allure of gaining recognition as "the best in the U. S." or "the best in the world"
is almost irresistible. Some may want public recognition;
others may want the private satisfaction of knowing that
they are the best. If you or any of your shooting friends have
these motives and possess talent in shooting sports, you
might be interested in the training opportunities offered by

the United States Army Marksmanship Unit (USAMU). The vast majority of world-class shooters in the U. S. in recent years have spent time training at the USAMU, which operates facilities and training programs to support the U. S. marksmanship effort in world competition. If you are interested, write a letter describing your goals and circumstances to Commanding Officer, USAMU, Ft. Benning, Ga. 31905. You will receive a personal reply and will learn how the great resources of the USAMU can be used to advantage in furthering your marksmanship ambitions.

There is intense satisfaction to standing on the winners' platform and being recognized as "the best."

11 Coaching

In terms of a national marksmanship program, the U. S. today lacks a sufficient number of trained coaches with the ability, interest, and means to develop shooters into world-class competitors. In a population as large as ours there are many potential world champions in almost all marksmanship sports. Holding us back in world competition is the lack of advanced-level coaches and, to some extent, the lack of a national training center for shooting sports and a mechanism to support individuals engaged in serious training. We can compete successfully against other nations who have these resources only if we develop similar resources in the U. S. Plans are underway in the NRA and among various private groups to foster changes that will improve our competitive position among nations. To do so is at least in the interest of national pride.

A major reason for the shortage of coaches is that there are very few paid coaching positions in the civilian sector. Almost all coaches who are paid for their work are in military marksmanship units or with collegiate teams, and collegiate coaches are usually military personnel on assignment with ROTC units, serving double duty as coaches of both the ROTC and varsity teams. There are exceptions, but they are all too rare.

We wish to extend our respect and appreciation, then, to the large number of civilians who donate their time to coaching civilian marksmanship teams in this country. Many work primarily with youngsters, introducing them to the sport, teaching them the fundamentals of safety and shooting techniques, and attempting to mold them into competitors. These coaches often work against severe limitations imposed by time, equipment, facilities, and finances. As job-holders in other areas, they sacrifice time and energy that they could blamelessly spend on themselves or their families. Given the limitations they face, they do a tremendous job and we have the greatest admiration for them.

In this chapter, however, we shall not focus heavily on coaching an individual or team at beginning or intermediate levels. That belongs in another book. Instead, we shall confine ourselves principally to discussing the strategies of coaching an individual or team in advanced stages of development, capable of competing seriously at national or international levels.

This does not mean, though, that the coaches of club teams around the country are outside our consideration. On the contrary, many of them have potential international competitors on their own teams. With proper coaching and guidance, those individuals might advance to world-class levels; often, the coach is the catalyst that starts the shooter thinking in this direction.

Throughout the rest of this discussion, let's assume that we're talking about adult shooters—individuals, usually 18 or older—who are capable of taking full responsibility for position development, training, mental preparation, etc. Given this, it is reasonable to ask the question, "Who needs a coach?"

The answer is that everyone, including a world champion, can benefit by having a coach. True, individuals can and have won world championships entirely on their own efforts, without the aid of a coach. But all would probably agree that their task would have been easier and their progress more rapid if they had had access to the *right* coach.

What makes a coach right? A very touchy question, that is. Even the most famous coaches in all sports are never sure exactly why they succeed. Is it because of something they do or say? If so, what? Or is it because they have the right material to work with? These factors can never be quantified and known with certainty.

But in shooting, the right coach is one who can work with, and to some extent for, the individual shooter. This makes shooting sports somewhat different from, say, football, where successful coaches often operate on the premise that the players work for the coach. In a sense they do, and authoritative coaching methods can be successful in championship football.

But shooting sports are different. A champion shooter is almost required to derive his intense motivation from his own inner being. By the time he reaches advanced stages of development, his style of approaching problems and training is often highly individualized. To attempt to force that individual to meet a coaches presumption of what "all good shooters are like" is to precipitate violent clashes of will and either demoralization or rejection. The role of a coach in dealing with a potential champion is a service role, a helping role.

Yet a coach cannot afford to be subservient or fawning. To be effective, he must be respected by the shooter. He must be perceived as strong, competent, resourceful, dependable, reliable. The shooter must feel that he can entrust the coach with intensely personal and private confidences and know that those confidences will be respected. He must feel that the coach will give him straight, honest answers to his questions; he must feel that the coach will give him tough advice, even painful advice, but that the advice is given only with the shooter's best interests in mind. He must know that when he needs help, the coach is there and can be relied upon.

Coaching a champion shooter is a difficult, demanding job, not because the coach has to do so much, but because he bears the responsibility of maintaining a very exacting relationship to the shooter, a relationship precariously balanced between authority and friendship. He has to win the shooter's absolute confidence and then maintain it absolutely. Not an easy job.

The most effective approach to a given shooter is almost always designed specifically for that individual, and a talented coach possesses the ability to intuit very early in the relationship what that approach should be. Some shooters need the support of a strong authority figure who imposes and demands a certain discipline; others need guidance through more gentle suggestion. Some shooters respond positively to wit and sarcasm directed to their errors; others are devastated by this approach. Some shooters will try to emphasize the "friends" relationship with the coach (something that must be carefully controlled by the coach, or he will lose his position of authority); others will avoid the coach except to talk with him strictly about the business of shooting. A coach working with a team of champion shooters has to be extremely resilient, capable of maintaining the best, most productive relationship with each individual.

Occasionally even the best coach will adopt the wrong approach toward an individual and find that the relationship won't work. If possible, it's usually desirable to sever the relationship and allow the shooter to find another coach. If this is not practicable, the coach must be extremely resourceful, careful, and firm in establishing the relationship on a new basis.

With a potential champion, the coach should operate with one purpose in mind—to help that individual win a gold medal. He should work just as hard at that goal as the shooter does, perhaps even harder. His primary function is to be a sounding board, a confidante and advisor with whom the shooter can clarify, discuss, and formulate his goals and his mental preparation. Regarding positions, the coach usually cannot tell the advanced shooter what he is doing wrong, or how to do something correctly; he can only tell the shooter when he is doing something differently or developing an obviously incorrect bad habit. To this end, he should be thoroughly familiar with positions and techniques in general, but also thoroughly familiar with the shooter's own individual position and techniques. In the latter case, he gains familiarity by detailed observation of the shooter and through reading the shooter's diary.

However, while the coach of a group must relate differently to each individual, he must also treat them all alike. This is not double-talk. It is simply a convenient way of saying that a good coach is completely impartial and grants no favoritism or special advantage to any member of the team. If he grants exceptions to team rules to one individual, he must grant the same exceptions to all members. He cannot impose requirements on one or two members, but not the others.

A coach coaches individuals but manages a team. "Team" is to some extent an ambiguous word. It can refer to the entrants in a specific event, or to the often larger group of individuals who practice and train together. But in either case, the coach should try to build a "family" atmosphere in which all members work together and support each other. There are various techniques for achieving this goal, but the following steps, in order, are a good basis. We'll assume that you're going to be a coach.

1. Organize the team to win. The organization must function exclusively to support the shooters in every respect. If the organizational structure creates delays or hardships or imposes additional duties on the shooters or in any way works against them, the organization is wrong. It should function to enable them to win, and it should foster and stimulate winning attitudes. Time spent improving organizational structure is well worthwhile, and organization should receive periodic review.

2. Build the team's confidence in yourself. You do this by hard work, mostly a great deal of advance planning and thought. Demonstrate that everything you do is to further the best interests of the team. Build absolute confidence in your integrity so that if a single shooter feels that something is wrong, he can come to you and you will deal with it in a manner that is fair to everyone and also effective. This requires a very strong commitment on your part. You

need to set the highest standards of dependability, honesty, integrity, dedication to and pride in the team, and then exemplify those standards without fail in your own personal conduct.

3. Establish goals and inspire confidence. If you were coaching the U. S. national team, for example, your goal should be to dominate shooting in the entire world. Your goal must be realistic, but it should be high. One effective technique is simply to announce the goal during a team meeting. Then write it down and display it where the members can see it. Some shooters may express astonishment that you've set the goal so high, and react initially with "We can't do that" or "I can't do that." Your response must be one of absolute confidence: "Yes, you can. And we will." If they have confidence in you, they will, in time, come to believe that your confidence in them is justified. They will adopt and work toward the goal themselves. Confidence is contagious among team members. You should establish goals carefully and then be the source of confidence for every member of the team.

4. Help each individual design his own most effective training program. This is based upon private discussions with each individual. Offer some suggestions, and if necessary impose some requirements in order to keep an individual from slacking off. Require the shooter to write out his program and provide you with a copy. To the extent possible, you should be with the shooter when he works in a training session. You needn't socialize with him at these times. You can use the time to observe, to become familiar with, his po-

sition and techniques; but, of course, be discreet about this: no one wants to feel that he's being stared at.

But on the other hand, everyone wants to feel that he's important enough to deserve your interest and attention. Your mere presence, with an occasional demonstration of interest, will serve to fill this need. Use these occasional private sessions to emphasize that the shooter is important as an individual, but also as a member of the team.

5. Protect team morale. This is partly a function of good organization and preparation, but it is also a function of selecting the proper members of the team. Occasionally you will be faced with a troublemaker, a rotten apple who infects the other members of the team with his whining, complaining, negative attitudes, or poor conduct. If you're coaching a club team at the beginner or intermediate levels, there's not much you can do about this except maybe try to change the offender's attitude, or perhaps cut him from the team as a last resort. But if you're coaching a potential championship team, you're justified in cutting the offender as a first resort. Such a person can quickly wreck the positive mental attitudes that are essential to winning.

One good way to approach the solution is to avoid an open or public dismissal. Have a conference with the offending party at a convenient time away from the other members of the team. Tell him candidly and forthrightly that he is being cut immediately because he is not contributing to the best interests of the team. Insist on a clean break, for such individuals will often try to convince you they will change for the better, only to take their negative attitudes underground and work against you in secret. Be firm, decisive, and decent about it, and you'll win the respect of everyone. Later, at the next team meeting, state simply that you have cut the offender from the team because he was not contributing to the team's best interest, then say no more about it, even if asked. Again, you win respect, and any resentments will usually be short-lived as the other shooters realize that you're working for the betterment of the team and understand that what you did was not necessarily easy.

Another morale builder is to recruit new members to the team who are potential major contributors. If possible, recruit them for try-out periods, then dismiss them if they fail to show enough potential. This is effective in several ways. It makes the established members feel a certain pride in themselves because it implies that they are elite, they have already "made the grade." It also stimulates them to perform well in the presence of the try-out. And it motivates the try-out and instills pride in him when he finally makes the team. This technique, it should be clear, is again partly a function of organizational structure and operations; and in addition to the above advantages, it ensures greater depth and longevity to the team over the months and years.

6. Prevent the shooters from becoming equipment conscious. Almost every team will have a few members who want to taste the forbidden apples of gadgeteering or experimental gunsmithing. No serious shooter should be involved in either of these pursuits. If at all possible, you as coach

should take full responsibility for gun testing, repairing, and tuning, though of course you don't have to perform these functions yourself. An expert gunsmith can be invaluable to a highly developed team, and if you have access to one there will be times when you love him more than you love your own mother.

If individuals use their own equipment, you can if possible make arrangements for all servicing, repairs, tune-ups, etc., to be done through you—that is, the equipment is brought directly to you and you make all arrangements with the gunsmith. Some shooters will balk at this, and even try to go around you, but make it a firm team policy applicable to everyone and you should have little difficulty. If the shooters use equipment owned by the team, of course, you have no problem in this regard.

Your purpose here is to prevent shooters from getting involved in equipment when they should be concentrating exclusively on their own performance.

You should expect mixed attitudes about equipment. One shooter will have performance problems which he can't recognize and will conclude that his gun is acting up. Another will shoot with a faulty gun and conclude that something is wrong with his performance. You have to be on top of these problems by knowing the shooters, knowing their guns, and having access to someone—probably a gunsmith—who has the knowledge and facilities to test a gun thoroughly and reliably. You should also be aware that shooters tend to follow the same patterns. Some will routinely blame their guns, some will routinely blame themselves when their scores begin to drop. This can be helpful knowledge, but it can also blind you to the fact that the shooter of either type will occasionally be right. Constant alertness is required.

7. Select match entrants on the basis of a ladder system. This has multiple advantages over having permanent first- and second-string teams. It keeps the level of motivation high, as each individual strives to bring his training scores up (or keep them up) to the level of the first-string team. It also ensures that at any given time, the best shooters in the organization are placed together to field the strongest possible first team. Also, it puts every shooter in the organization on an even footing and avoids any hint of favoritism from the coach. Everyone has an even chance to make the top team every day.

There are exceptions to this. If an individual has won a berth on a national team by virtue of his scores in national trials, he has earned that spot and it is his despite the fact that other members of the team may have better scores in the days prior to the final competition.

Another consideration sometimes arises in international competition where there may be multiple events but a country is limited to registering only a fixed number of individuals. In current Olympic competition, for example, a nation can have only four rifle shooters who then compete in three events: the 50-meter 3-position, the prone, and the air-rifle matches. This poses a selection problem because one person could easily win the trials in one event but be mediocre or worse in the other events. Whether this person would be the best selection would depend on the strengths and weakness of the other selections. He may or may not be the best choice, and in circumstances like these, the ladder system should not be the only criterion.

8. Relieve the team of as many responsibilities as possible in planning for competitions. As coach of a championship team, you or your assistant should take full responsibility for submitting team entries and fees, drawing up a travel schedule, reserving lodging, arranging for meals, etc., and for giving a detailed schedule or plan to each member of the team. Assign training routines for those who will be left behind. Arrange an early organizational meeting at the match site to determine if everyone arrived safely with the necessary equipment, and to make last minute announcements and changes.

If travel is to be across international borders, make sure every member of the team has the necessary paper-work completed and that the permits to carry firearms have been issued to the team.

Make lists and more lists, and check and double-check. Your job is to prevent inconveniences and delays, and to relieve shooters of any unnecessary responsibilities so they can devote themselves to maintaining peak mental and physical condition for the match. Trips to matches should be fun and characterized by a positive, trouble-free tone, at least for the shooters. If you're successful in maintaining this atmosphere during a trip and an important match, it usually means that you've suffered many sleepless nights and headaches and have made a Herculean effort to conceal your own fatigue and irritability that arises from dealing with seemingly endless details and minor problems. But that's part of a coach's job.

9. Protect your shooters at matches. If your team has a good chance of winning, there's a good possibility that opposing teams, particularly at certain international matches, will attempt to distract, harrass, or intimidate them by challenging the legality of your equipment, challenging your schedule, challenging your scores, and using a whole host of devices to upset your team's equilibrium.

   Keep your shooters away from these scenes as much as possible. Send them somewhere else. Then fight it out with the challengers, using the rulebook as your weapon. If you know the rulebook backwards and forwards, and know that everything about your team is legal and in order, you will win your case and, to some extent, turn the tide by embarrassing your challengers.

   Tactics of harrassment are unsportsmanlike and usually counterproductive. You should never use them yourself, but you should be prepared to defend yourself against them from certain quarters.

   On the other hand, you should also protect your shooters from illegalities commited by opponents. If you truly suspect that opposing shooters are using illegal equipment or procedures, immediately contact match officials and issue a challenge.

10. Develop a strategy in advance of a match. Before you leave home base (or before other competitors arrive, if you're hosting the match), you need a clearly-formulated strategy for winning. Usually this means a plan to get the best results from the shooters you're working with by entering individuals in their strongest events in the correct order. For example, suppose a rifle event

consisted of prone matches the first day, 3-position matches the second day, and air-rifle matches the third day.

Now suppose that your Shooter A is strongest in prone and 3-position, and your Shooter B is strongest in 3-position and air-rifle. Quite probably you would avoid scheduling Shooter A on the last relay of day one and the first relay of day two, and Shooter B the last relay of day two and the first relay of day three. This schedule would force them to compete with a minimum amount of rest between matches. On the other hand, does either Shooter A or Shooter B perform best in the morning or the afternoon, or best in the first or last relay? Work these strategies out in advance, and then be prepared to be flexible, as the next item illustrates.

11. Refine your strategies based on what you learn at the match site. The possibilities here are so vast that they defy complete discussion, but here are a few examples.

Say you arrive at the range a day or two before the match and have an opportunity for a walk-around inspection. Carrying a lighted cigar and watching the smoke, you learn how wind affects different firing points differently. The range in front of one point is particularly well protected from the wind. You decide to position your best shooter on this point and give him a better chance to post the high individual score.

You study the range house and realize that some firing points are closer to the main traffic flow of spectators and range officials. You try to be assigned other points, or you place your best shooters on your assigned points where there is the least amount of traffic and distraction.

You learn that firing will take place in three relays and that your principal individual opponent has already opted for relay number two. If your shooter with the best chance of beating him would be intimidated by the opponent's score, you place your shooter on the first relay. If, on the other hand, he would rise to the challenge of a high opposing score, you'd place him on the second or third relay.

On practice day you learn that one of your shooters has a gun that is beginning to lose accuracy. You decide that he cannot use an unfamiliar gun and produce a score as high as your team alternate, so you withdraw the shooter with the bad gun and enter the alternate.

You observe range officers during a match and notice that they are creating conditions favorable to another team. You confront the officers or challenge their procedures to higher officials.

You observe the scoring officers and notice that one seems to be incompetent or biased. You alert other coaches and challenge the officer, perhaps moving to have him disqualified.

In short, during a match you should be observant and working to see that everything is honest and fair, and to gain every legal advantage you can for your team. Anything you can do to these ends will pay dividends, sometimes important ones. Especially in close competitions, the coach's alertness and resourcefulness can mean the difference between winning and losing. You cannot plan all of the right moves in advance. They must be developed on the spot, much as a basketball coach develops a winning strategy for the final two minutes of a tied basketball game. The situations are similar in some respects. In a close basketball game, the players do not win in the last two minutes by themselves; the coach wins, by developing a workable strategy that gives his players the advantage. In marksmanship too, the decisive moves are often made not by the shooters, but by the coaches.

Part of your strategy should be to keep your observations to yourself. If you learn of a certain advantage to be gained by using the range, the relays, the procedures in a certain way, don't reveal this knowledge to your opponents, certainly, and don't reveal it to members of your own team unless there is a good reason for doing so. If your shooters have confidence in you, they will do what you tell them without question, believing that what you're doing is best for the team. There's no reason for any team member to know that one firing point is better than another, or that he was purposefully placed on a relay before or after an opponent. Sharing this knowledge may actually be damaging to the team. It should be yours, and yours alone.

12. Allow your shooters to take full credit for winning. You may have nurtured a shooter to maturity and supported him through bad times and worked feverishly to gain him an advantage during a match and in fact made him a success through almost superhuman effort on your part. But you should always allow him to take full credit for his achievements if you wish to continue being a successful coach. Taking credit yourself will destroy morale and inspire antagonisms faster than anything else you can do short of personal betrayal. You'll do just as poorly if you remind the shooter in any way at all of how much you've done for him. Congratulate him on his achievement, sincerely, and then forget your

efforts in his behalf. In the long run, you'll get your share of recognition and credit for producing a whole stable of champions, and then the nature of your accomplishment will be clear to everyone.

These are by no means all of the responsibilities of a coach, but they are the primary ones. Perhaps a quick review will be useful.

A. Work with, and to some extent for, each individual.

B. Earn the shooters' respect, maintaining a balance between friendship and authority.

C. Approach each shooter individually.

D. Your whole purpose is to help that individual become a champion.

E. Treat each member of the team in the same fair and honest fashion. Avoid favoritism.

F. Coach individuals, but manage a team using the following principles.

1. Organize the team to win.

2. Build team confidence in yourself.

3. Establish goals and inspire confidence.

4. Help each individual design his own most effective training program.

5. Protect team morale.

6. Prevent shooters from becoming equipment conscious.

7. Select match entrants on the basis of a ladder system, except under special circumstances.

8. Relieve the team of as many responsibilities as possible in planning for competitions.

9. Protect your shooters at matches.

10. Develop a strategy in advance of the match.

11. Refine your strategy based on what you learn at the match site.

12. Allow your shooters to take full credit for winning.

We hope this discussion has aroused some interest in marksmanship coaching. Obviously it is a difficult, time-consuming, challenging job, perhaps equally as challenging as the task facing a shooter who has set his sights on a high-level championship. Many people mistakenly believe that a good coach must himself be a championship shooter, but this is not true. He or she needs to have some competitive experience in shooting and needs a broad, detailed understanding of marksmanship performance; but the coach may actually be better off for having no personal record to protect and no highly individualized shooting style which he feels is "right" for everybody.

Aside from a sound technical knowledge of shooting, a good coach at the advanced level needs a real interest in people and an intuitive ability to understand what makes individuals tick, what drives them, what their needs are, what they respond to. He also needs administrative skills, the ability to think clearly, set goals, formulate plans, and execute them effectively. He needs to be resilient and resourceful and unselfish.

Is it worth it? We think so, and we would be remiss if we did not mention some of the rewards of coaching. Aside from the obvious rewards of seeing one of your shooters win a coveted championship—which is not a daily or even a frequent occurrence—there are many more subtle, frequent, and even more meaningful satisfactions that come from working with young men and women. Coaches can have powerful and very positive influences on their players. Probably the results stem from the coach's psychological role in his players' lives. Good coaches are perceived by players as friends, even intimate friends; yet at the same time they are perceived as powerful authority figures. Therefore they may become role-models, sources of style, values, precepts, and attitudes, in a much more influential way even than parents. If a coach provides a more positive role-model than the young person has had before, his influence can be admirable. Many athletes have testified to this, often crediting their coaches with "turning them around" and "getting them on the right path" not just in sports, but in life itself. Experiences such as these are almost entirely responsible for keeping many coaches involved in an otherwise difficult and demanding profession.

We are not talking here about the old cliche that "sports build character." This may or may not be true. (Sadly, in corrupted amateur sports such as Division I collegiate football and basketball, it may be an inversion of the truth.) We are talking exclusively about the coach's personal presence vis-a-vis his players. He can stand for values of honesty, decency, integrity; he can demonstrate the value of clear thinking, planning, and organization; he can exemplify dedication, perseverance, and the worthiness of sacrifice for some meaningful reward. If you are a gifted coach and have the psychological impact you should have on your players, you can not only teach them how to win in sports, but influence them to be better, more productive, happier people. Even if you don't produce a champion, this can make all the effort and all the work worthwhile.